As I See It

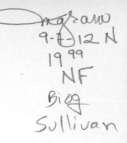

As I See It

My View from the Inside Out

Tom Sullivan

HOWARD BOOKS
A DIVISION OF SIMON & SCHUSTER, INC.

NEW YORK   NASHVILLE   LONDON   TORONTO   SYDNEY   NEW DELHI

Howard Books
A Division of Simon & Schuster, Inc.
1230 Avenue of the Americas
New York, NY 10020

First Howard Books hardcover edition September 2012

HOWARD and colophon are trademarks of Simon & Schuster, Inc.

For information about special discounts for bulk purchases, please contact Simon & Schuster Special Sales at 1-866-506-1949 or business@simonandschuster.com.

The Simon & Schuster Speakers Bureau can bring authors to your live event. For more information or to book an event, contact the Simon & Schuster Speakers Bureau at 1-866-248-3049 or visit our website at www.simonspeakers.com.

Designed by Kyoko Watanabe

Manufactured in the United States of America

10   9   8   7   6   5   4   3   2   1

Library of Congress Cataloging-in-Publication Data

Sullivan, Tom.
   As I see it : my view from the inside-out / Tom Sullivan.
      p. cm.
1. Blind—United States—Biography. 2. Blindness—United States.
3. Self-perception—United States. I. Title.
   HV1792.S855A3 2012
   362.4'1092—dc23
   [B]
                                                    2011047298

ISBN 978-1-4516-6351-8
ISBN 978-1-4516-6353-2 (ebook)

*To all the family, friends, and mentors who
helped me create an inside-out view of the world
that has given me better than 20/20 vision*

Contents

CONTENTS

As I See It

Prologue

I'VE NEVER MET a person who was ugly unless they wanted to be.

I've never seen my wife's face, but I've listened to the sound of her smile.

I've never looked at a rainbow. *Color* is just a word.

I see life inside out, rather than outside in.

I'm sixty-five years old, and you'd think by now this old dog had learned all the new tricks necessary to be a reasonably successful human being. I've had a wonderful life; and, quoting Lou Gehrig, I think I'm the luckiest man on the face of the earth.

There's my wife, Patty. We've been married just over forty-one years, and honestly she's the greatest gift this man has ever been given. And then there are my children, Blythe and Tom, sensational people. I have friends in high places, and a few of them are characters that inhabit some of the lower ones, mostly Irish pubs.

My career has spanned just about everything there is to do in the creative arts. My health has been perfect, and it has allowed me to maintain a pretty good level of overall physical fitness for somebody who's now a senior citizen.

So why, for the first fifty years of my life, was there this thing that kept nagging, pulling, and needling its way into my sense of self-worth? Why did I believe that for some reason my essential being—my aliveness—was less than yours? Why did I think that being blind truly was a disability? Why? Because I didn't have the wisdom necessary to see my own existence differently—to understand I needed to start perceiving life from the inside out, rather than the outside in. Why didn't I turn the paradigm of my blindness upside down, and why did it take me so long to come to terms with who I was and how I belonged in the world that's principally made up of those of you with sight?

> Why did I believe that my essential being was less than yours?

I think it's a pretty profound question, and I'll try to answer it in these pages, but maybe a story—and I love stories—can best illustrate what I'm talking about.

Patty was excited as we sat on our patio enjoying a wonderful glass of Brunello, the great red, rich Italian wine whose grapevines cling to the rugged Tuscany countryside.

"You'll love it," she said. "We'll start in Rome and take in the Sistine Chapel, where the great master touched the world with his frescoes. And then on to Florence, where many of Michelangelo's sculptures are housed in various museums. And just think of it, Tom. Blythe will be with us and her friend Amy. You remember Amy, Blythe's girlfriend who's fluent in Italian and has an advanced degree in art history? For you and I to share this trip with our daughter—what could be better?"

In that instant of my wife's ebullient enthusiasm I wasn't sure how to respond, and certainly the choice I made could not have been worse.

"Listen, Patty," I tried to say, "looking at frescoes and studying great art doesn't mean much to a blind guy, you know?"

I smiled, trying to make light of what I was saying, but got only icy stillness from my wife.

I plowed on. "Listen, why don't we do it this way? I'll take Sully [Tom Jr.] with me. We'll go to Scotland, play the great golf courses, and meet you in London for some terrific theater. Now that's a vacation, right?"

I'll bet we've all had those moments when the more we talk the worse it gets, and clearly that was what was happening to me. Patty wasn't buying it a bit.

"Tom," she said, "don't you think it's important for you to at least understand visual art? I know you can't see it, but certainly learning about it is critical for you to grasp. I mean, you are an artist yourself, so shouldn't you be paying tribute to the great masters? And anyway, I don't want to go to Italy without you. All that good food, wine, ambience."

I suppressed sighing outwardly and accepted my fate.

So there we were in Rome standing in the Sistine Chapel. Now, I don't want you to think that I was being completely insensitive. I mean, I felt the gravitas of the place, the holiness of the most important church in the world, the seat of the Pope. I have a strong faith, one that I've written about in many other books. In fact, my relationship with God is the most important element in my life. But on this day Patty, Blythe, and Amy were studying Michelangelo's astounding work and were appropriately in awe.

On the flight over, I had read *The Agony and the Ecstasy* and was deeply moved by the struggles of this remarkable genius, but as to grasping the visual dimension of his artistic achievements, well, simply put, I was totally blind.

After a couple more days of sightseeing in Rome, we moved on to Florence. To enter the square means to once again be under the influence of Michelangelo. There is the *David*, an immense piece of Carrara marble that our friend Amy told me made it seem as if the king is alive.

It was a rainy afternoon as we entered the Uffizi museum, and I was already beginning to have sore feet as we moved from room to room and my boredom became more intense. Actually, it wasn't just boredom that I was feeling. I was feeling sorry for myself. Here we were looking at sculptures done by the hands of the great man, but for me the experience was vapid, empty, disconnected, meaningless; and, as in other moments in my life, it's fair to say I slipped into depression and like other times questioned God as to why I was blind. Why was Tom Sullivan denied the experience of beauty? Why had I been chosen to go through life unable to appreciate man's most creative accomplishments?

I don't think Patty picked up on what I was feeling, and our daughter, Blythe, was so absorbed in what she was seeing she certainly wasn't concerned about her father. But Amy sensed what I was going through. I will always be grateful to our friend Amy Frederick, this wonderful young woman, for what happened next.

She noticed a man dressed in formal daytime clothes and believed he must be someone important to the museum.

"*Signore*," she said, in her beautiful Italian, "my uncle *lui cieco*—is blind. Is there any way . . . ?"

There are ultimate moments in a person's life, experiences that transcend all others. For me, this moment—this singular hour on the clock of life—changed my life forever.

I was taken behind the ropes and allowed to touch the works of the artist. Under my hands—the hands that had been my eyes on the world—the masterpieces came alive, and in a moment of beautiful clarity I realized that I understood every nuance he had hammered and chiseled into the Carrara marble.

> This singular hour on the clock of life changed my life forever.

I touched *Moses*, feeling the fullness of his beard, the tablets of the Commandments under his arm, the set of his chin, as if he was saying, "I will bring the people of Israel out of bondage." There was the high forehead, the angle of his shoulders preparing to move, to reach for freedom.

And that theme of freedom was carried on in the slaves, the supplicant *Dying Slave*, with his hand behind his head, dropped shoulders, downcast eyes, all in preparation for his death. And then the *Rebellious Slave*—powerful! I could count every muscle, every striation on his remarkable body as he stood poised to fight.

And then there were the mother and child. Mary holding the baby Jesus, not to her breast but away from her body extending him to us, as if she already understood that someday she would offer him up on the cross in order to forgive our sins.

I was crying now, uncontrollably, the tears pouring down my

face because for the first time I grasped, in this place—indelibly etched in my memory forever—that I was no longer really blind because I was seeing Michelangelo's work inside out, as he had seen it in its creation.

I was no longer really blind
because I was seeing
Michelangelo's work inside out.

The curator was by my side. *"Signore,"* he said softly, "I wish I could take you to Rome and show you the *Pietà* so that you could understand the full circle of the master's gift. You know it is Mary holding Jesus, her only son, after they crucified him. So much love. I believe you would feel it in the tips of your fingers and in the depth of your heart."

In his eloquence, the curator of the Uffizi museum had summed up what it was that I had been searching for all my life. I had ached to discover a formula that would allow me to believe that my perceptions could be as valuable as yours. I had needed to justify my own existence, to come to terms with why I had been committed to a life in the darkness, and now this discovery, this personal renaissance had come about.

From that day to this and on through the rest of my time on earth I realize that my way of looking at the world will remain unique and, yes, unusual. I'm sure that in God's essential plan I was chosen to be blind, and after many years of struggle I've come to terms with that remarkable truth (more on this in chapter 8).

Along my journey I have learned much that I hope to pass

on to you, but for now here's what I want you to understand: blindness is the best thing that has ever happened to Tom Sullivan. Would I like to be able to see? Certainly; to see the beauty of nature in all of its forms, the faces of the people I love, and the myriad colors of a sunset. I'd love to play center field for the Red Sox or catch a touchdown pass from Tom Brady and the Patriots. But I have not only become content with my lot, I now celebrate my own uniqueness with closed eyes but a completely open soul.

The joy in writing this book is in my knowing that even though I quite likely will never see as you do, I might just be able to change your perceptions and broaden the possibilities for your own appreciation for the grace God has provided us with and for the life we're so blessed to live.

So, take a look—as I see it—inside out, rather than outside in.

CHAPTER 1

In the Mind's Eye

A FEW YEARS AGO, I had the chance to meet a remarkable man named Michael May. At the time Mike had just won medals in the Winter Paralympics in multiple ski events— the downhill, the giant slalom, and the Alpine combination. He also had been crazy enough to ski faster than any person without sight, clocking a time on a downhill course of over sixty miles an hour.

Okay, so my friend Mike is a little crazy, but he's also a genius. He probably has done more for the development of technologies for blind people than just about anyone in the world. His breakthroughs in voice actuation and adaptations of devices like the iPhone and iPad have made it possible for guys like me to operate professionally on an equal playing field with my colleagues. A Stanford graduate with an IQ that's off the charts, Mike was actually born with vision, losing it along the way, so he has a perspective on both what it means to see and what it means to be totally blind.

Recently, he became a major story in newspaper and television headlines when, due to an amazing breakthrough in oph-thalmology, Mike got a good deal of his vision back. Imagine that. After having lived much of his life in darkness, Michael May was once again able to see—to see his family, to see his beautiful wife, to see nature, to see a computer screen. All of it—the world—now was open to him, and yet it was all too much. Too much for this remarkable brain to compute.

The pictures taken in by the camera we call the human eye just didn't make sense against the pictures he had evolved during his life as a blind person. Was a face a face of someone he knew? He couldn't tell right away. Could he ski as freely as he did when he was blind, as he struggled with depth perception and real-object identification? My friend arrived at the remarkable conclusion that the world he experienced being blind was a world he understood. The new presentation based on his renewed capacity to see was, in a phrase, much more complex than even this remarkable man would have expected.

I believe Mike's story definitely frames the amazing separation between the world you understand with your eyes and the world I've taken in, not only through four other senses but through the collaboration of all my external antennae into a picture my mind's eye can absorb and turn into my personal reality. I will spend a lot of time in this book talking about the capacity of the senses, but I think it's just as important to discuss the limitations.

For me to have a true picture of anything material, I generally have to shrink it down to something I can touch. So, as an example, when my children were born I remember absorbing every inch of their bodies with my fingertips, smelling their heads, feeling their newborn breath on my cheek, analyzing what was meant by any cry issued from these infants around their needs. Like you, I counted every finger and every toe over and over again, just to make sure they were all in place.

And then there was my sense of the world. Until I began traveling for a living, the globe and its countries only existed on a large tactical relief map with lines and bumps that defined oceans and mountains I touched at the school for the blind. Though I knew all about dogs, cats, and even horses, based on my childhood experiences that were very up close and personal, lions, tigers, elephants, alligators—all of Noah's two-by-twos that entered the ark—were completely foreign to me because I couldn't see them. I didn't know them.

During the 1970s in the Soviet Union a number of experiments were done with blind people trying to find out if they could learn about color through touch. Certainly after a while the heat given off by various shapes could be deduced as light and dark by touching various materials. But it really was only an exercise because color is only a part of the visual spectrum.

And what about understanding large spaces, like when I would go to Red Sox games or when I sang in the National Cathedral or stood in the middle of a football stadium preparing to sing the National Anthem for the 1976 Super Bowl? In that moment of unbelievable American pride, with my voice echoing around the vast stadium, I came to another truth about what it meant to be blind: I would always struggle with large spaces. The size of things, the depth of things, the dimension of things that you know so easily with your eyes. For me, the world is only three-dimensional if I can touch it and hold it. An object becomes real in

For me, the world is only three-dimensional if I can touch it and hold it.

its dimension only when my hands send the message to my brain that makes my knowledge of whatever the thing is complete.

As a little boy, I loved erector sets and building blocks, and I remember so well how my friend Billy Hannon and I built forts and houses, all of them in miniature, of course, but all of them something I could touch and then understand. My favorite place to go on a Saturday was the Children's Science Museum in Boston. Even back in the fifties the museum had a policy of allowing blind kids to touch as many things as possible, and thanks to them my perception of the world and many of the creatures that live in it took on real shape.

> Is my picture of life broader than yours or narrower in scope?

Is my mind's eye—that is to say, my picture of life—broader than yours or narrower in scope? When I'm confronted with a problem that is complex and I need the help of the smartest people I know, what do I do? I have found that the basic life secret is to go talk to children. They don't lie, and their perceptions are far more intuitive and to the point than adults'.

I recently spent time with a third-grade class at our local elementary school and discussed this fascinating idea. First they asked me basic questions like did I understand color, how do blind people dream, did I know what my wife looked like, did I wish I could see—the things I've been asked all my life. And then we got down to the conversation about how they perceive the world and the pictures they have of things that were only appropriate when understood from the perspective of external vision.

A little girl asked me simply how I could tell who she is from someone else. I first talked about how special her voice was, and then I told her that I could smell chocolate candy on her hands.

"Yes," she said, laughing. "I had a Twix bar at recess."

I told her about when we shook hands I noticed how soft and long her fingers were and that when she gave me a hug I happened to touch her hair and remembered that it was very thick.

"What color is it?" she asked.

"I think it's blond," I said.

"How do you know that?" she asked, amazed.

"Oh, I just know," I said. "You kind of learn how to connect voices to people."

A little boy at the back of the room piped up. "I guess I use my eyes for almost everything, but I think you're telling us that we should make our picture better, right?"

"That's right," I said. "When I picture a flower, as an example, I know what it feels like to touch a rose and then to smell it. I know what the air is like on a beautiful spring morning when you can almost taste the moisture and how I feel when I walk through a beautiful garden. All of that is part of the picture I have of not just the rose itself but the environment it lives in."

"Wow," my little girl friend said. "So, it isn't just what you see, is it? It's what you sense?"

"That's right," I answered, really excited that they were getting the idea. "The world is not just about what you see from the outside, but it's about how the mind can give you a more complete picture by using all of your senses, all of your intelligence, and all of that very special thing we call *instinct*. Does anybody know what *instinct* is?"

A little boy in the second row said, "It's how you know whether or not you're going to like some other kid. It's a feeling you get."

"That's right," I said. "It's just a feeling, and you should always trust it."

I loved my time in the class with the kids, and it brought me back to connecting the dots with the prologue of this book. Remember, I told you the story of my trip to Italy and the amazing opportunity I had to touch some of the great works of Michelangelo Buonarroti and how under my hands the artist's genius came alive in a far more personal way than you could ever experience with your eyes.

So, is my vision for things twenty-twenty? Well, certainly not if we discuss it only in external terms, but if we frame the world I operate in from what I like to think of as my own dimension of inside out, my mind's-eye picture of life, though different, has no boundaries. Because, along with the information I take in, my imagination expands all of my understanding. And, ah, the power of the imagination. I think I'm a writer because I'm able to transport myself virtually anywhere I want to go on the wings of my imagination.

> My mind's-eye picture of life has no boundaries.

I once wrote a novel called *Together*, where my principal character was a sighted mountaineer climbing high in the beautiful Rocky Mountains. From my imagination I discussed fall colors, along with a rainbow he watched after a summer shower. I wrote about how far you could see from the top of a fourteener and how cars down below became like toys played with by a child.

I'm not trying to tell you that I understand the world as you do, but I've learned to adapt my mind's eye to create a commonality with you. And my passionate desire as I write this book, I think, is that you allow yourself to journey inside the dimension of your mind to broaden the picture of life as you know it. The perspective all of us can gain by mutually understanding the pictures drawn either by the eye or by the mind can only benefit all of us in our capacity to engage with each other as human beings.

Though there is so much I wish I could see, there's also so much I already am blessed to know through the mind's eye, inside out.

CHAPTER 2

Our Common Senses

IT'S ALMOST MORNING—that time of suspension when night gives way to day. I too am beginning to shed the darkness, exchanging it for a different kind of brightness, a luminescence created by four magnificent messengers: the senses—touch, smell, taste, and sound. Though my eyes are not a contributor, I do not feel lacking in perception.

My wife, Patricia, slumbers on beside me, and I am comforted at the sound of her rhythmic breathing. It is tempting to reach out and take her into my arms, but on this morning it is not necessary to be demonstrative with my love. Her smell is as enveloping and completely reassuring as the warmest embrace. It is all familiar, all woman, all Patty, all mine. She is my greatest treasure, my eyes on the world, a gift from God.

From habit I roll onto my back and stretch out my left hand, and he is right there. The jingle of his collar as he rises from the floor tells me that my guide dog, Edison, has been waiting for me to signal that it's time for best friends to enjoy our morning run along our beloved Pacific Coast. This special confluence of land and ocean is my favorite place on earth. It's where I go most days—rain or shine—to be renewed; and it is through the antennae of my senses that I reconstitute the simple but essential daily joy of being alive.

> Through the antennae of my
> senses I reconstitute the simple but
> essential daily joy of being alive.

Dog and master quietly sneak their way out of the room and go downstairs without disturbing the sleeping woman. The coffee pot is on a timer, and that first taste of joe is as delicious to this morning runner as a complex burgundy. With the dog's harness and leash in place and my running shoes on, we step outside to assess the morning. My nose defines the weather report. *June gloom*, it tells me. The fog is in. Probably won't lift until early afternoon. There is a pervasive moisture in the air, but rain is unlikely at this time of year.

Hey, what's that? Somebody cut their grass yesterday, and Mrs. Martin's early-season roses have just begun to open. I hear the *whack* as the paperboy—maybe the last of his breed—throws papers from a bike as he passes by and I call out a morning hello.

Just before we leave the house my voice-actuated clock tells me that it is 5:15, so I know that it's still more dark than light. No problem; Edison guides me perfectly. His senses are far more capable than mine. He pauses at curbs as we move through the neighborhood and easily traverses around garbage cans and other objects, never failing to notice any loose, wet leaves that just might cause his master to slip or fall. In all of his concentration he is completely focused on our mutual goal.

We move down a long hill, our pace quickening almost to a sprint, and reach the top of a cliff, finding the path that will take us down onto the sand, and we hear it—the rhythmic pulsation of the Pacific's surf as it rolls onto the land. I stand, for a moment transfixed by the sound, counting the seconds of the waves' intervals. Today they are at nine seconds between the breakers. That means low tide—perfect for running. The roar is like a cannonade in a war zone as sand and surf compete for their place on God's terra firma.

At high tide the sound is very different. Outgoing sand jousts with incoming waves like two great heavyweights in a championship fight. The punch is dull but devastating, thudding into the body of the land.

Now the big German shepherd eases me down the narrow path. Pebbles slide under our feet, and occasionally I hear the sound of an animal as it hurriedly skitters away into the bushes. Eventually, we arrive on the sand. I strip off my shirt and shoes, wanting to run barefoot close to the ocean in order to feel its salty mist on my shoulders.

You know, there are eleven different kinds of sand on my beach, from fine granular to pebbled sedimentary rock that has been ground into submission and pounded into sandy pulp by the centuries and timeless ocean swell. Tidal change, weather conditions, curvature of the earth, and the capricious nature of the sea have actually created fifteen different kinds of waves I'm blessed to listen to and understand, though their differences can often be subtle. But if you listen—ah, if you listen—their various signatures will become clear.

At the three-mile point in our run there is a restaurant that sits up on the cliffs above our beach opening at 6 a.m., and the smells of freshly brewed coffee, muffins, bacon and eggs, and other breakfast delights come drifting down on the ocean's breeze and blend with the scent of eucalyptus, lilac, and mock orange blossoms. These are the condiments, as it were, to the taste of the ocean. As I breathe in during my exertion, what is initially smell becomes taste, and it is all clean and pure in an ever-changing state of delicious delight. Seaweed, kelp, single-cell life, and, yes, even death are necessary parts of this most magnificent sensory ambiance.

The dog and I are running faster now, and I take note that he breathes four times to every one of mine. As I hold his harness, he planes off, galloping, and I imagine myself as a water skier on the end of a towrope. I'm turning back time as I race faster than I ever could have imagined at this stage of my life.

And now there is an audience that is witnessing our performance—the sound of the sea lions barking us home on the rocks at the end of our beach. When I begin to hear them, I know that we have probably about five hundred yards to run. My heart is pounding in response to our efforts, and I feel the first rays of the morning sun gloriously touch my shoulders. Coming to a stop, I breathe in large gulps of sea air, warmed by the early morning sun. I bend down and remove the big dog's harness and leash.

"Okay," I tell my friend, "let's go." Man and dog charge whooping into the ocean and swim out beyond the surf line. It is quiet out here—completely quiet two hundred yards from shore—and I roll onto my back allowing the waves to toss me to and fro without a thought, without a care.

Labs are better in the water than German shepherds, but

Edison has learned to swim, and though I'm not sure he loves it the way I do, he accepts the morning ritual with equanimity. Eventually, I reach out and take my friend's collar and allow him to swim us back to shore. We dry off, and he guides me home, both of us looking forward to breakfast with Patty and sure that our day has gotten off to a *sense*-sational start.

> Our day has gotten off to a *sense*-sational start.

I like to think of myself as the conductor of a sensory orchestra with the capacity to point my baton to a soloist or call for the playing-together of the whole ensemble. True, my senses are always working, so I suppose it's not quite like giving the downbeat and expecting the orchestra to play at my command, but I don't think my analogy is very far off base. Standing on the beach at the end of our run, I'm able to isolate a seagull's cry or the bell buoy ringing five miles out in the bay.

It's not hard to separate smells and distinguish, for example, one flower from another. Though I'm not an expert, I understand that visually a person can become laserlike in terms of their focus and attention, so I suppose it's a lot like having individual volume controls in the way our senses take in and inculcate the information to our brain center, defining in a nanosecond what we know as input, knowledge, or information.

Just as I've heard many of you with sight say that there are no two people who look exactly alike, I don't think there are two people who sound alike. The imprint of the human voice is as varied as the imprint of appearance, and the ability to read vocal intonation is a fantastic tool to have available. How often have you listened on the telephone to someone's hello and known exactly where that person was emotionally coming from? People are not aware of how much they give away concerning their mood with just that first simple hello.

And handshakes—boy, you can learn a lot from those. Let's consider the different types. There's the person who gives only the fingertips when they shake. Here we have the human being who doesn't really want to know or engage with any other. Then there's the rotating shake. This is someone who believes he is superior and must always be on top in every business or personal setting. The cruncher clearly communicates "I'm stronger than you," and he almost seems to take pleasure in breaking your fingers. And what about the pumper? Now, this for me is the confusing person. Some pumpers are all about being really terrific people who are delighted to meet you, while others are hiding behind bravado to mask what's really going on inside—usually insecurity. And what if a handshake leads to a hug? There are two kinds of basic huggers: upper body, usually offered by the fingertip shakers, and total huggers who I want to believe really care.

I think that maybe eye contact is overrated. When I meet a new person I know exactly whether they're uncomfortable with my blindness just by listening to the angle of their voices. When they don't make visual contact with my face, I understand that it's going to be difficult for me to contact them on any kind of personal basis. I've learned to listen to the way someone sits in a chair. Are they leaning forward, interested? Or does their voice suggest they might be dropping their chin, bored with our conversation? Am I hearing them sigh or move around with anxiety over our communication? I listen for all the quirky tics that people have—drumming their fingers on the desk, quickening their speech, how they deal with distractions. All of it feeds into the information gathered by the senses and provides me with—you guessed it—a major element of what we believe is our instinct.

In my work with Edison, the guide dog, I'm fascinated by his capacity to understand immediately what I'm feeling on any given day. When I'm tense he tries to work harder to ease my concern. When I'm joyous about a particular day or the experience of being with my family, he's looking for a tennis ball so he can join the game. If I'm quiet because I'm working on a project, he senses my intensity and becomes completely passive, seeming to grasp the importance of what I'm doing.

I suppose the amazing thing about my life with the senses is that even at this stage I believe I'm still evolving, sort of fine-tuning the orchestra and becoming even more perfect in my pitch. Let me say it this way. I'm grasping nuance and continuing to understand subtlety, constantly working to create a broader-reaching sensory panorama, and most importantly learning to turn on each sense and then amp up its volume.

Again, I credit Edison with teaching me what's possible in the potential of the sensory dynamic. Someday I hope I can

> I'm learning to turn on each sense and then amp up its volume.

hear as well as he does, and though I know my olfactory sense of smell will never equal my friend's, I'm getting a lot better at understanding what delicacies Patty's preparing in the kitchen as I sit in the living room looking forward to the dinner we're going to share. And let me make a note about awareness. Even though you rely principally on your vision to gain information, I'm sure that your ability to improve your sensory awareness is readily available.

I've known a number of friends who have lost their sight somewhere along the way during their life's journey, and within just a few years their acuity to utilize their other senses has increased by quantum leaps. When my children were young we used to play a game called "What's Mommy Doing?" Blythe and Tom would sit on my lap, and we would work together to figure out, just using their senses, what was going on in the kitchen. Was Patty working on the cutting board preparing a salad; and if so, what dressing was she making? Were we having chicken, beef, or fish as a main course; and what delight was she preparing for our dessert?

What I'm trying to say in this chapter is that the senses can provide us with an infinite level of possibility. It comes down to a choice to either turn on or turn off your sensory aptitudes. I can only promise you this: turning up your senses can only improve your quality of life. And isn't that what we all want—a better quality of life that allows us to share with those we love?

CHAPTER 3

Labels

AS A PERSON that's blind, I can't avoid the idea that I live in a world of labels and that I'm labeled by everyone as "the blind guy," but I really want you to understand that though that's my reality I have worked diligently to avoid, to abdicate, to throw away any fundamental engagement in labeling others or accepting categorical labels myself. Oh, sure, I name things. That is, I label my clothes in Braille so I don't go out looking like a rainbow with colors that don't match, I label my CDs so I know what music I can listen to, and certainly I'm aware that it's important to check the labels on food or medicine or anything you buy that might have a shelf life; but that form of labeling is just naming, identifying, informing. It is not categorizing.

And from the beginning of recorded time we—hominids, *Homo sapiens*—we've conveniently categorized; and when we practice an ultimate negative labeling, our categorizations have brought about acts so heinous, so cruel that even the words *genocide* or *holocaust* cannot adequately portray man's worst nature when applying labels in their ultimate distortions.

To label means not taking time to explore—not investigating the uniqueness that is clear and implicit in all of us. Because no two of us are made exactly alike, our differences should be cel-ebrated, rather than labeled; or even if we label someone, it ought to be in recognition of those qualities that make them special. The label of admiration when applied to the elements that separate you from me, is, I believe,

> We reflect the best of each other, as the moon reflects the light of the sun.

the vehicle that allows us to turn our experience with one another into our own personal growth. Our appreciation for another person increases the possibility of development in ourselves. We reflect the best of the other, as the moon reflects the light of the sun.

Consider your relationship with your children. It's so much fun when you get a chance to observe parts of their personalities that reflect the best of who you are. My daughter, Blythe, is one of the most spontaneous and enthusiastic people you could ever know, and along with that joy she also is extraordinarily organized. If you want a party, ask Blythe. She'll make it happen. If there's a ski trip to Colorado for our family, just let her do everything. It works out perfectly. That's exactly the way I tend to operate, probably because as a blind person I have to be organized just to survive, but the shoe still fits. Blythe and I operate from the same place.

Then there's my son, who has become a far more competent musician and songwriter than his dad. When I listen to him play, he has the same appreciation for R&B music that I developed during the sixties and seventies, and he also has super ears when he's mixing the tracks. The apple doesn't fall far from the tree, and there's a commonality in how people who share do things.

When we label, we narrow our focus, we dumb it down, we reduce our nature to something simplistic and frankly very boring, and most importantly we limit our vision. Externally, when we have vision loss, we call it names like *glaucoma, macular degeneration, retinitis pigmentosa*. But when the loss of vision occurs inside out, we call it *bigotry, prejudice*—we call it *labeling*.

Though all of this may seem somewhat abstract, it makes all the sense in the world (no pun intended!).

It's amazing for me to look back over the six decades plus of my life and realize that my battle over labels began before I was even able to be cognizant of the problem. I was born three months premature and became blind because too much oxygen was pumped through an incubator, destroying the retina. The irony of my circumstance was that had I been born three years earlier, I would have been dead, because scientists had not yet created incubators, and had I come into the world six years later, the chances are excellent I would have been able to see, because doctors had refined the amount of oxygen provided to an infant. So, maybe, just maybe, I came into the world at exactly the right time.

Anyway, my parents brought me home, and when they realized that something was wrong with my eyes they took me to an ophthalmologist, who at the time was considered the number-one doctor in the field. With absolute insensitivity he said to my father: "Mr. Sullivan, your child is blind. Institutionalize him."

Bang.

The institution he committed me to, at that moment, wasn't a place of safety surrounded by high fences. I was being predestined to spend my life in the institution of labels.

27

Blind.

The word seared on my parents' brains and programmed them first, foremost, and always to keep their little blind child, Tom, safe. Always protected. In this context, when did I begin to understand the label that had been placed on me? I find it amazing as I search the recesses of my mind for early memories to note that though I heard the word *blind* applied to me by many people—aunts, uncles, siblings, friends of my parents—it was not something that hung around my neck like an albatross. The bottom line is that my parents kept me safe and built a world in which I was the center, operating through my other senses with limited contact in the outside world. In fact, though my parents placed me in a school for the blind I really didn't begin to wrestle with the label until I was confronted by the cruelty of a child.

The word *blind* was not something that hung around my neck like an albatross.

I've told this story in another book and also used it fictionally in one of my novels. I mention this fact because obviously this experience became profound as I worked to develop a positive self-image.

Because my father owned Irish pubs frequented by some of Boston's great athletes, baseball became an early passion for me, and my hero was Ted Williams: Number 9. The Splendid Splinter. The great left fielder for the Boston Red Sox. My da had given me a Louisville Slugger bat autographed by the great man, and I treasured that piece of old hickory.

Down the street where we lived there was a Little League

baseball field, and on many spring days I would be in my back-yard surrounded by a chain link fence, listening to the sound of kids playing the great American game: the crack of the bat on the horsehide ball, and the pop as young players caught the ball and worked at their throwing skills. How I wanted to be part of all that. How I wanted to be in the world, outside the limitations of my fence.

What was available to me was my imagination, and I spent days with a portable radio sitting on the back steps, tuned to WHDH 850, the station that broadcast the Boston Red Sox. As the Hall of Fame announcer Curt Gowdy did the play-by-play, I would pick up rocks from the ground, throw them up in the air and try to hit them with my Louisville Slugger bat as if I were really playing in Fenway Park. On one pristine May afternoon, I got lucky and hit a pebble with all my nine-year-old strength. It felt like I had just parked one over the Green Monster, the left field wall in Fenway. I ran around my enclosure and slid into an imaginary home plate, exuberant, excited, proud of my accomplishment. But I wasn't alone. A little boy who had been on his way home from the Little League field witnessed my home run trot.

Kids can be amazingly cruel.

"What's the matter, kid?" he said from outside the fence. "Are you blind?"

In my innocence I did not sense the sarcasm in his voice. "Yeah," I said. "I'm blind."

"Well," he went on, "that's a stupid kind of game, and I think you're a stupid kid."

All I wanted was to play with him, to have him embrace me as his equal, to be his friend; but the label of blindness eliminated any possibility of establishing open communication.

"That's a stupid game, and you're a stupid kid."

He followed the statement up with a chant that still rings in my ears. He chanted. "Blindey, blindey, blindey! Blindey!"

I picked up rocks from the ground, hating him, wanting to hurt him.

"Blindey!"

I threw them at the sound of his voice, but he simply stepped out of the way and continued to throw my label directly into my face.

"Blindey!"

Eventually, he got tired of the game and went away.

I sat alone on the tire swing in the corner of my yard and cried my eyes out, understanding for the first time that I was being categorized—not just named or identified but categorized—as different, less than, a leper, a pariah.

It's so easy to look down on someone because of their labels, rather than look up to someone because of their qualities. All bullies—and that's certainly a topic today—come from a place of personal insecurity. A child picks on another because of some deep-seated crisis and inferiority complex. This child didn't even know me—who I was, what I thought. He couldn't imagine how much I felt or dreamed—how much I wanted to be his friend. All he knew was that I was blind, and that was enough to cast the stone and identify the label.

Blind.

Over the years I've never forgotten this experience, but as I've grown older and maybe wiser, I've figured out in context some issues that this kid was manifesting. First, I learned years later that this boy was the neighborhood bully, not just picking on me but lauding his size and strength over many other neighborhood boys. This kid was a failure in school, got into drugs, did some time in the slammer (jail, that is), and to the best of my knowledge has never found the path that has led to his own happiness.

Frankly, I don't really care if he ever experienced joy in his life, but I'm fascinated with the fact that most people who label others as inferior are people who operate in this manner because they're not happy with themselves, or they're insecure or paranoid.

The undercurrent in the Nazi extermination of Jews arose from their basic fear that Jewish people were too smart, too capable, and would, in fact, dominate the Aryan race. They called it "purifying the breed," but essentially many historians believe it arose out of the people's insecurity and was capitalized on by the persuasive leadership of Hitler—a madman.

The same argument could be made right here in America concerning the Ku Klux Klan. The KKK smugly believed that they were superior in every way to the black man. People of color should remain slaves. They were inferior and should be owned by their masters.

Ethnic and racial superiority are the most glaring and obvious applications of labels, but all forms of handicaps also carry with them the stigma that allows people of limited minds to compartmentalize and pigeonhole anyone they view as different. I say, vive la différence! Society will never grow, cannot expand, will not become truly inclusive until we eliminate the convenience of labels.

There is a flip side in this conversation that ought to be acknowledged. Identifying *yourself* with a label can be a terrific asset. When we see a person in the armed services in full dress uniform we feel a sense of pride; and when that soldier, sailor, marine, airman, or coastguardsman feels proud of themselves, it shows through in the spit-and-polished way they wear their service's symbol.

Jerry Rice, the greatest receiver in the history of the National Football League, was meticulous to a fault in the way he put on his uniform to play games on Sundays. He told me

> Identifying *yourself* with a label can be a terrific asset.

that getting his uniform on just right was an external part of getting his internal preparation for the game right. I believe they go hand-in-hand. A label can work symbolically if it's supported by an internal commitment from the person to wear it well.

Historians tell us that George Washington, the father of our country and first president, was—according to John Adams— truly presidential in manner and bearing. (And remember, Adams went on to be the second president of our burgeoning United States.)

Over the years I've come not only to accept the label of my blindness but to appreciate what it has brought me. Let me make it clear, I've worked hard for every bit of success that has come my way, but in the crucible of disability those moments that occur based on the blend of work and ability become even more important and fulfilling as you work to build self-worth. As you've read in earlier chapters, I've enjoyed a world of senses that many of you never have taken the time to appreciate. (Whoops. Now I sound like I'm labeling anyone who can see. Sorry about that.)

In one way or another, this entire book is really about manifesting the positives in all of us; and in the case of my being blind, I've learned to make the most of the label. So, labeling is a mixed bag—potentially horribly negative but sometimes the most magnificent of positives.

Labeling is a mixed bag—potentially
horribly negative but sometimes
the most magnificent of positives.

I spent ten years working for *Good Morning America* on ABC, and I can't even begin in these pages to talk about all of the stories I was blessed to do on people in all walks of life who were beating the odds. But one maybe makes the point better than any other. A number of years ago, Joni Eareckson Tada was an athlete who loved hiking, tennis, and swimming. In an instant, her life changed when she broke her neck in a diving accident. She languished in pain, despair, and depression until she found strength in her faith, and also in the discovery that she was a remarkable painter: by holding a brush in her teeth, she creates pictures that now sell all over the world.

The way in which we apply labels, along with how we live inside our label, will have much to do with the question of our success or failure as human beings.

CHAPTER 4

Beauty

IT'S SAID THAT beauty is in the eyes of the beholder, but if that old adage is really true, we are limiting our view of the world to only an external and subjective perception of what is beautiful. Unless we're discussing inanimate objects—trees, flowers, oceans, rock formations, etcetera—beauty has to be a quality that shines out from within.

Here's a warm and endearing example of what I mean.

A pal of mine who lives on our street owns Bella, an English bulldog with wrinkles deeper than the Grand Canyon, a pushed-in face, and a nonexistent tail—a dog whose parts seem ill-formed, out of place, put together as a joke of creation. But to her master and to me, Bella is one of the most beautiful animals we have ever encountered. I love the way she shakes and quakes when we meet. Her loving passion is enhanced, made even more beautiful by the snuffling and snorting of her somewhat asthmatic breathing. She loves my friend absolutely, and her loyalty is unquestioned. In short, to those who love Bella, she is beautiful.

I was working for *Good Morning America*, the ABC morning show. My job back then was divided into two parts. Most of the time I covered stories of people who were beating the odds, proving constantly to our audience that anything was possible. But sometimes when my fellow correspondents were overwhelmed with important world events to cover, I would get assigned to the celebrity beat. That was just fine for me because I was in show business and knew a lot of the people I was sent to interview. One afternoon the producers called me in and told me that I was going to do a piece on the hottest new star of the time, Bo Derek.

Beautiful Bo had just finished the blockbuster movie *10*, where she is supposed to be the perfect-looking girl—a ten. And from things my friends told me around the water cooler, that was the truth. In fact, a lot of the crew guys sarcastically noted that it was a little ridiculous to send a blind guy to interview Bo.

"What's he going to get out of that experience?" they said.

Okay, when you're a young professional you are more than willing to rise to a challenge, and I decided that my first question to Mrs. Derek was going to be a doozy.

When the cameras rolled, I leaned forward in my chair and said, "Bo, people tell me you're a perfect physical ten, but I can't see you. So what I want to know is, why should I like you?"

Looking back at the moment I realize I certainly was an arrogant young reporter. First of all, why should she even care if I like her? And second, it was a trick question. I was setting her up to fail. Boy, was I surprised by her response.

Bo began to cry, and she said, "Isn't that the truth, Tom? Nobody looks at me beyond the physical. They don't care that I love my husband or that I'm committed to animals and their well-being. They don't know that I have an interest in politics or that I love to read. All they know is that I'm somebody that looks good running down a beach in a bathing suit."

I understand that physical beauty is clearly in the eyes of the beholder. No question. And this may best be reflected in the personal approach of artists and the way in which they paint or sculpt their perception of beauty. Until his soul is discovered, even the greatest artist is at best creating his sense of beauty as a caricature. Physical beauty alone is vapid, empty, uninteresting, lifeless.

Remember the introduction to this book? For as much as I was moved touching the great works of Michelangelo, I knew that the beauty of the sculptures could not compare with beauty seen from inside out. For all of us this could be best illustrated when we consider the innocence of children. They are truly transparent, guileless, unencumbered by complex life agendas. We all recognize their beauty, no matter their origin, race, or creed. It is rare to meet anyone who does not embrace and appreciate the beauty of a child.

> The beauty of the sculptures could not compare with beauty seen from inside out.

Often at about three o'clock, after a long day writing, I walk outside my front door and listen to the sounds of children coming home from the school a couple of blocks away. Their joy—and most significant, their laughter—touches my soul and reminds me that I need to become so much more like them, open and transparent.

As I write this chapter, I find myself considering the question of whether I have regrets about not being able to see physical beauty. Certainly, on my morning runs along the ocean near my Southern California home, I regret not being able to study the panorama that Robert Louis Stevenson described as the most unique confluence of land and sea.

Now, he was talking about an area a little farther north— Carmel, California, to be precise. But my confluence of land and ocean ain't bad at all. I've told you about listening to the waves, drawing in the smells, touching the sand, but I wouldn't be honest if I didn't admit that I'd love to look out on that remarkable vista and enhance my appreciation for the beauty through sight. Certainly, I'd love to see the smiles of my children and the look of absolute love that comes from my German shepherd guide dog, Edison.

But I've come to terms with all that. If I have a truly ongoing regret, one that pulls at my heart on a regular basis, it's that I have not been blessed to see my wife's beautiful face enhanced by the love we've shared over more than forty years of marriage.

Here's a blind man's picture of Patty's external beauty.

I love it when I hug her and her head fits conveniently just under my chin. I'm six foot two and a half, and Patty claims to be five foot four and three-quarters, a perfect fit. She's curvy, womanly, but through years of commitment wonderfully physically fit. She hates her hair, saying that it's too thin, but I love the way it tickles my chin when she snuggles into me. Her face is unlined, and when I touch her cheek, I feel no wrinkles under my fingertips, and when I've kissed a tear away at a sad moment, I'm aware that her eyes are deep-set, large, and penetrating. Her voice reflects her consistent life optimism. It is warm and round, contralto in tone that registers joy most of the time. When she laughs, nothing is held back. It comes from her gut, meaning a joke is truly shared. And when she tells me she loves me, I know that it comes from the depths of her being and is reflected in every moment we treasure along life's journey.

When the poet wrote, "How do I love thee? Let me count the ways," we were really being told that the task would be impossible. Beauty in its highest aspect is understood when it is driven by love, and the moments of beautiful reflection occur for me in some very specific experiences.

It's Sunday morning around 6:30 a.m. I always get up before Patty and take Edison for his walk. No run on

> Beauty in its highest aspect is understood when it is driven by love.

Sundays. That's my day to be at home with Patty. I make the coffee and bring my wife her first cup as she's getting out of bed. The hug we share is warm, as the night smell of her sleep wafts into my nose. I hold her for a moment, saying good morning and kissing her on the eyes. Maybe I do that because her eyes are my windows on the world.

Back downstairs she opens the Sunday paper and reads me the headlines. If there's a story that interests us, we share it and talk it through, but mostly we speak quietly about private things—our children, my prospects for work, a house deal that Patty the Realtor is trying to close, friends we've recently been with—and sometimes we just sit silently, enveloped in a beautiful cocoon of love and intimacy.

Now it's the end of the day, and we take Edison for a walk along the cliffs at sunset. He's not working, just moving with us at heel, so Patty is the guide. I hold her arm or rest my hand on her shoulder, and she is always pitch-perfect as she navigates us along. She tells me that she doesn't even think about my blindness anymore.

"Being blind doesn't mean anything," she says. "It's just part of you, and I suppose it's become part of me."

Part of you. Part of me. The beautiful synergism of a loving couple.

Later, we decide to go out for dinner, and without discussing it we order the same thing from the attentive waiter. Now back home, the day ends as it began, under the covers, and we are held close in the relationship that can only be described as beautiful.

There is no moment more beautiful than when you have the opportunity to meet people who have been married a long time—fifty years or more—and observe them as even more in love than they were when they were young. This was made wonderfully clear to me when I met Jim and Mary MacElderry. Jim recounted their first date attending a movie and standing in line during a rainstorm. Mary's feet were getting wet, so Jim bent down, took his shoes off, and replaced her wet sandals with his own waterproof oxfords. Even though they were a little big, the gesture of love still touches me whenever I think about it. And, by the way, while he told this story they were holding hands, and I could tell by the sound of his voice that his eyes never left a face he still found irresistibly beautiful.

So, beauty can be appreciated in the expanse of an ocean's panorama or in the smallest delicacy of a winter snowflake. It can be presented in the eyes of da Vinci's *Mona Lisa* or in the sculptures of Michelangelo. Claude Monet may almost bring a flower to life, but it is necessary for all of us to experience the delicacy of a rose close up and in person.

And so, beauty is truly experiential, and to understand it,

appreciate it, a person has to live and—again, as the poet says—to walk in beauty. To appreciate beauty, we must be beautiful ourselves. External beauty may be celebrated, identified, or acquired, but internal beauty—beauty inside out—needs to be defined in the way we interact with others. I believe this is clearly a choice, as the soul, the essence, of who we are was defined in our basic creation. Just consider the innocence of a child and realize that in a first smile, a first "Mama" or "Dada," a first hug from little arms, there is no guile or intent; there is only love expressed from a soul of perfect inner beauty. We will change along the way, scarred by our life experience, but reaching for the absolute, the place from where it all began, clearly must be our goal.

Beauty is in the eyes of the beholder and in the senses, but far more important, it is found and expressed in an open soul and a true heart. Though I'm blind to many things, beauty, understood inside out, provides me with absolute twenty-twenty vision.

CHAPTER 5

A Life of Interdependence

WE GLIDE THROUGH a world of silence interrupted only by the almost imperceptible sound of snow falling on the branches of the aspens bordering the ski run known as Mary Jane Trail in Winter Park, Colorado. Although I can't hear her, I know my daughter, Blythe, is never more than a foot away, skiing in the tracks I make as we float down the mountain.

It is a perfect Colorado powder day. *Champagne*, the locals call it, light enough to feel almost transparent as we move through it. In the silence our breathing seems to take on an aspect of gigantic proportion, like a movie with the audio turned up. Breathe out as you sink into the turn. Suck in the much-needed air as you rise, gliding through the powder. Keep your shoulders over the tips of your skis and press your hands down the hill. Turn your skis and follow your knees, they say, but in powder every motion needs to be exaggerated.

I feel the snow fly over my shoulders and whoop with delight, believing I am virtually weightless in my downhill flight. We come to a narrowing of the trail and Blythe's voice cuts in. "Hold the next turn, Dad. Traverse the hill. Go, go, go, go. And turn, and turn, and turn. Bumps coming. And turn. Slow down. Traverse the hill. And turn. Let 'em run, Dad. Let 'em run." She has just guided me through a transition to the lower part of the hill. And again, she is quiet and I am free.

I hear the sound of the chairlift below and drop into a tuck, bringing my skis together with my butt nearly touching the snow. Thirty, forty, maybe even fifty miles an hour. I feel the wind but do not hear it as the zephyr is absorbed by the sound-proofing of the snow. Forty exhilarating seconds later, Blythe's voice cuts in again. "Coming up on your left, Dad."

I switch the poles to my right hand with my left arm extended. In a seamless connection of love and skill, our hands join and we are skiing as one, turning together in an intimate ballet reserved only for those bonded in trust. This is the ultimate in blind skiing. Her hand moves up and down to indicate when I should turn, and I read the degree and intensity of the movement according to the effort she is making. Edge and release, glide and slide. We ease into the chair lift line with the precision of a docking in space.

"What do you think, Blythe?" I ask. "Should we go up again?"

"Are you kidding, Dad? This is the best powder of the season. Or are you getting too old and your legs are fried?"

A challenge from my daughter.

"Hey, if you can handle it, no problem. Let's go."

Halfway up the ascent, we're not quite as sure. It's now a full-fledged Colorado snow dump, and I figure they'll close the mountain before we reach the top. Blythe's voice conveys her apprehension, although she expresses it lightly.

"It's a whiteout, Dad. I'm as blind as you."

We're not fooling around anymore. Both of us understand that, and we wonder if it might be better to stay in the lodge at the top of the mountain and have a hot chocolate. But no, we're the Sullivans, undaunted and maybe a little foolish. We grope our way to the takeoff point of the trail with conditions still getting worse.

"Hey, Blythe," I say, a little of the macho worn off, "how bad is it?"

"Dad, I can see the trees on the side of the run, so we won't hit anything, but I can't feel up or down."

I understand exactly what she means.

In a whiteout, all perspective is gone for people with sight, and you literally might be moving across the hill just as easily as you might be headed straight down. And yet there is a real excitement in this moment because I know exactly where the vertical is. Skiers talk about a mountain as having a fall line—a slant where gravity and inertia pull you left or right across the hill. My special kinesthetic feel lets me know exactly how to compensate and keep us headed right down the middle.

For the first time in our mountain sharing I will guide my daughter. "Keep your eyes on the trees, kid. I'll do the rest."

Mary Jane Trail has five pitches on the way down separated by flat areas where you can let your skis run. I know them all as if I could see them, and on this day the combination of a daughter's eyes and a father's feel allows us to navigate through the storm in total safety. The loving interdependence makes the experience unforgettable. What a story we'll have to tell in the warmth of the après-ski bar.

The amazing ski experience I shared with Blythe is a loving snapshot, a microcosm of a core value I learned through the process of developing vision inside out. I believe that from the smallest single-cell creature to the most complex man and woman on the planet, we are all interdependent; and when we figure that out, maybe, just maybe, we'll find the equanimity necessary to—how can I put it?—get along, nation to nation, person to person—and even more important, family member to family member.

From the smallest single-cell creature to the most complex man and woman on the planet, we are all interdependent.

When you really think about it, this premise applies to everyone. How can a surgeon do his job without a gifted nurse who places a scalpel in his gloved hand at just the right angle and at just the right time to complete an operation? The building of anything can occur only when the contractor acknowledges the significance of the architect's plan and the talent of the subs who work for him. On a movie set, actors assume successful characters only because everyone else, cameramen, soundmen, grips, makeup, and hair, along with stage managers and gifted directors, come together in an interdependent way to guarantee the successful execution of a movie we enjoy in a darkened theater.

From the time of my diagnosis as a blind infant through the attitude of protectionism developed by my parents and society believing that the best way to educate a blind child was through a system of isolation, I felt imprisoned, trapped behind high walls that separated me from the outside world. I was cast as a dependent human being who would always be forced to depend on others if I was to find a place in life. This overriding belief fostered in me an out-of-control need to be independent. And so, I was always taking chances. Do you remember when you were a kid and you did daredevil stuff? Well, in order for me to gain some form of involvement with neighborhood children, I was always the kid who would take on any challenge, even if I was risking life or limb.

In Boston (in West Roxbury, to be precise, where I grew up), like every kid, I waited for that first big snowfall. The time when schools were closed and a foot of snow made it possible for children to be outdoors in a winter wonderland. Just down the block from where we lived there was a high wall over an alley at the back of a building. I actually don't know why it was there, and I can't remember exactly how high it was, but to my nine-year-old brain—especially because I was blind and couldn't assess the real circumstance—the drop might have been from the top of a mountain.

No matter. Blind daredevil Tom Sullivan—and isn't it ironic that fifty years later I helped Ben Affleck make a movie of the same name—was willing, no, even eager, to be the first person to leap from the top of the wall and find out just how deep the snow really was.

I remember standing on the edge with my knees quivering because I had no real sense of how far I was about to fall. Was it two feet? Six feet? Ten feet? Or a mountain crevasse? I didn't know. All I was sure of was that I had to win friends in this moment of risk. Years later, I went back to find out exactly how high the wall really was. It turns out the drop was about five feet, but back then, in those seconds, hanging in space, fear was overcome by need—the need to be one of the gang, a sharer in the adventure of life. The leap of faith was more than worthwhile.

Now, you'd think that a person would outgrow this need to risk in order to gain approval, to put his life on the line, to say to anyone who would listen, "I'm independent." But I suppose I haven't really changed.

A couple of years ago I went to New Zealand and took the highest bungee jump in the world: 330 feet off Skippers Canyon Bridge. Why? I don't know. The skiing stuff I just wrote about? I ski too fast. I go over bumps that are much too big for a guy in his sixties. I have a tandem bike that I ride with friends willing to compete in triathlons, and I admit I'm constantly forcing them to be competitive, to go faster, to try harder. Is all of this obsessive? Compulsive? Stupid, even? Or just the expression of need by someone who is still saying, "Hey, take a look at me. I'm independent"?

Now, I have modified my own psychology. With the passage of time, I've come to believe in the essential concept of this chapter, so I don't want to give you the wrong impression. I'm convinced we are all interdependent, and it's reflected in every element of how we operate. Consider the exquisite nature of creation: every creature is dependent on another to survive, whether it's as a food source or a source of love. Every creature shares an interdependent relationship with another.

> Consider the exquisite nature of creation: every creature is dependent on another to survive.

For me this truth plays out in my reliance on a guide dog. It is hard for me to find the words that can adequately describe what it's like to work with a guide dog. I have been blessed with four of these magnificent animals.

Dinah, my first dog, was an astounding golden retriever, whose gentleness and talent took me around the world during the years I worked for *Good Morning America*. I've written about Dinah with my friend, the actress Betty White—the hottest girl in show business, who, by the way, likes it when I call her a girl—who lovingly took Dinah into her life when my dog had to retire. When Nelson, a joyous black lab arrived, Dinah could not accept the idea that she was no longer my working partner, and so she went to live with a Golden Girl.

Now, these two Golden Girls—woman and retriever—spent five glorious years together. When Betty and I wrote the book *The Leading Lady*, I think Betty summed up our relationship with Dinah very well. She said, "Dinah taught Tom to grow up and taught me to grow old."

Clearly, teaching is a major element in what makes us all interdependent. In the chapter on senses, you read about my morning runs with Edison on my California beach. Consider the interdependence of this process. I'm the master. I'm calling the shots. I mean, deciding where we're going to run, how fast we're going to go, how long we're going to run. But it's Edison that keeps me safe and provides me with—and I'm using a phrase now that may on the surface not make sense—the freedom of interdependence.

Back to the microcosm of skiing. When Blythe was calling our turns on the first run down the slopes of Aspen, I was completely dependent. Then when she released me to ski on my own and was only there in quiet support, I experienced the closest moment of true independence a blind person could ever be allowed. And then, seamlessly, she took my arm, and we skied as one, making our turns and trusting each other in a balletic expression of complete interdependence.

Right now as we struggle with an unemployment rate of nearly 10 percent across our country and we acknowledge the near collapse of American banking, we face a seismic event as our nation is forced to determine that its economy is forever linked to global prosperity. No longer can we simply create more goods and assume that the world wants what we make. We're being forced to reassess our sense of interdependence. The future will not allow us to posture ourselves as isolationists.

Though many Americans resent the growing power of, say, nations like India and China and their influence over our economic futures, we'd better figure it out, and that applies just as critically to my friends, the 54 million people with disabilities I care so much about.

It is not just the responsibility of society to come to terms with the rights and privileges of those of us coping with disability. We also must develop the character to recognize how to be interactive in the application of our own interdependence.

Among my friends with disabilities, many of them have built up walls of resentment that block their recognition of interdependence. I think the scarring of their dependent lives has placed emotional barriers on the capacity to acknowledge the reality of genuine interdependence. The movement for real freedom in the disabled community will only find effective direction when we put aside our hang-ups over our sense of dependence, along with our unrealistic need for independence.

I love golf. In fact, if you asked Patty, she'd tell you that I'm obsessed with the game. Okay, maybe I'm telling you more than you need to know, but when I'm struggling with my swing, there have been nights—oh, around three o'clock in the morning—when Patty has awakened to see her husband in his underwear with a golf club in the middle of our bedroom working on my chip shots. Not only does she think I'm crazy, but she isn't really happy with the divots in the rug. I'm just kidding. I haven't divoted our carpet yet, but I do swing the golf club sometimes in the middle of the night.

I own every conceivable golf device ever made to improve my swing and technique. Our garage is a veritable pro shop. Between the stuff I've bought and the things I was given by golf companies when I was more of a celebrity, Patty figures that someday there'll be a garage sale that could, oh, let's say, put a down payment on a house for one of our kids. Anyway, you get the point.

Right about now, you're probably asking yourself how a blind person plays golf. Well, it's a lot like skiing and like working with Edison. It's because of two young men who commit so much of their time to my obsession. My son, Tom, and a new American citizen from South Africa, my friend Luke Manthe, are my eyes on the green. And the job is complicated. For those of you who aren't golfers and those of you who do play the game and might be interested, here's how we do it.

When we come to the tee on, let's say, a par four dogleg left, meaning the angle of the hole is from right to left, my coach, whether it's Luke or Tom that day, and I first discuss the wind direction. Then we pick the ideal shot we're going to play.

He'll say things like, "Tom, I want you to keep this ball down the left side of the fairway. Let's hit a draw against the wind, meaning turning the ball right to left in the air. I'm going to line you up down the right center. I want you to close your feet a little and get your left hand over the top of the club so that you can hit a hook."

Then he tees up the ball. Now he holds the club on the exact target line he wants the ball to fly, like pointing a rifle. I place both hands on the shaft of the instrument and step out, keeping my feet, hips, and shoulders square to the line of flight he has chosen. After he places the club behind the ball, *voilà*, I try to hit the crap out of the ball.

With a little luck, I'm 240 or 250 yards down the left side of the fairway leaving a short iron of 110 yards to the hole. For me, that means a pitching wedge or a soft nine-iron. We talk about it, line up the same way, and I hit the shot.

When we arrive at the green my skill set really kicks in. Let's say the ball is thirty feet from the hole. We walk from the ball to the hole, allowing me to read the green's surface with my feet. I decide that the ball is going to break a foot from right to left and confirm that idea with Luke or Tom. Now they line up the putt, and with a confident stroke I make it for birdie.

I'm laughing as I'm writing because that's certainly not always the case, but you understand.

Like skiing, like my work with guide dogs, as in the case of my marriage to Patty and my relationship with my coaches on the golf course, my life has become a state of interdependence, and that state is a marvelous place to be. I do want to point out that I'm not trying to say that all of us shouldn't be striving for success. We all have the right to gain competitive advantage based on our talents, hopes, and dreams. But a process that fosters only the selfishness of personal goals will continue to splinter our relationships, person to person and nation to nation.

> My life has become a state of interdependence, and that state is a marvelous place to be.

In professional football, the divas on a team are the wide receivers, the guys who catch the ball thrown by a strong-armed quarterback. These people rarely have to block for a runner, and even when the play begins they're set off the line, away from the other team members. One of my best friends is Mike Shanahan, former coach of the Denver Broncos, and now the head man with the Washington Redskins. Over drinks on many wonderful evenings, he's talked about how these diva players see themselves outside of the team chemistry. Sports pages are full of stories about these guys who just can't get along. They want the ball, whether it's in the best interest of the team or not. Consequently, they place their need above the team; and coaches, like my friend, lose their hair in frustration.

So, being blind has given me the insight to understand the absolute compelling need for interdependence. I understand that I can't do it alone, and the really cool thing is that living as an interdependent person allows you to consider others as a critically important part of your life. This idea of mutual interdependence is a core value when talking about life inside out. It comes down to an appreciation of the other, and in that appreciation we gain the ability to study others from an inside-out point of view. Our relationships become more personal because they're tied to our own success, a success that can only be gained from an inside-out appreciation for who you are and how it affects me.

There's a wonderful story that illustrates the premise of this chapter in a charming way. Some clinical professionals undertook a study to find out just how independent children from different cultures really were. A checkerboard was arranged with one checker set in the center, offering two children an equal chance, one move at a time, to get to the other side of the board. When Americans played the game, no one won because the two children involved continued to move the checker back and forth without achieving a goal. In the case of the Japanese kids, because of a culture developed around team survival and interdependence, surprisingly, these kids worked to allow one of them to win on behalf of both with no prompting from the researchers. Interdependence requires sacrifice, but the result is clearly beneficial.

CHAPTER 6

Turning Points

THERE ARE MOMENTS in life that clearly determine our destiny. These are seminal experiences that carry with them the power to affect change, to determine our attitude, our future, and often our relationships with those we love.

All of us can point to these moments, and some of them are common to everyone: your first friend, that kiss you stole from a girl with braces somewhere out behind your neighborhood school, a sport, academic or artistic success, graduation from high school and then college, your first job, falling in love, getting married, having children, watching them grow, seeing them leave, the sadness of divorce, the loss of a loved one, and your own mortality.

I hope it might be instructive for me to talk about the turning points that directly affected my life as I look at it inside out.

The first critical turning point was one I wasn't even aware of. It was the ophthalmologist's pronouncement to my parents that I was blind and should be institutionalized. Obviously, this set them on a path to protectionism and limited my capacity to engage in the normal activities common to a little boy with sight. But every turning point has a silver lining, and I suppose we find that valuable stuff when we realize that the human capacity to adjust is limitless.

So, how did little Tom adjust to his early life in the dark? Through my imagination. And what was the vehicle that allowed my fantasy to take flight? Old radio.

> The human capacity to adjust is limitless.

Since I was born in 1947, and since most people didn't get their first twelve-inch black-and-white television until the mid-fifties, radio was what I listened to for the first seven or eight years of my life. I was right there with the Lone Ranger and Tonto as they pursued Butch Cassidy and the Hole-in-the-Wall Gang. I flew into space with Tom Corbett and Flash Gordon. The Shadow wasn't the only one who knew what lurked in the hearts of men; even at an early age I was able to figure out the mystery presented on NBC radio. I was there as the Gang Busters worked to bust Al Capone, and I even took an interest in daytime soap operas like *Our Gal Sunday*, *Ma Perkins*, *The Guiding Light*, and ironically, *Search for Tomorrow*, a soap opera that forty years later became my television home for a little while.

Radio not only expanded my language skills, it sparked my creativity. My father got me one of the first reel-to-reel tape machines—I think it was a Revere—and I began to make up radio shows using anything I could find around the house to create sound effects. Cellophane became the way to depict a raging forest fire. Curtain rods were swords that allowed Sir Lancelot to vanquish the Black Knight. Taking my shoes off and sitting on the floor created all kinds of sound opportunities—the galloping of horses, the striking of a baseball with a bat, or even two guys boxing in a heavyweight fight. Though I had been denied the gift of sight, the inside-out joy of my imagination took me anywhere I wanted to go.

You know how some kids say they have an imaginary friend? Well, I did even more than that. I had an imaginary gang. Tom Sullivan's Gang, to be precise. The gang was committed to fighting for what was right and bringing the bad guys to justice, and so many of the stories I made up with that old tape recorder mirrored the radio shows I loved.

My early turning point was labeling and loneliness, but it was overcome, or rather, turned into a positive, through imagination that developed a positive self-image.

I've told you the story of the little boy who called me "blindey" and brought my label into a clear and painful focus. What I didn't tell you was the result of this turning point. As I sat on the tire swing in the corner of my yard crying, I became competitive; competitively angry. Today I believe there are two kinds of anger destructive and competitive—and I think all of us could use a dose of the latter. Life is not easy. It's not a picnic. And when you face a turning point of rejection, your human spirit needs to galvanize itself around the idea of competitive anger. It was in this state of anger that a concept was born that led me to the next critical turning point.

When you face rejection, your human spirit needs to galvanize itself around the idea of competitive anger.

I was living in my fenced-in backyard. A small world within the big world turning on its axis out there, beyond the fence. I was a blind child inside a limited space, but I came to understand that someday soon I would have to break out of my enclosure and risk all to be part of the big world.

Now, there's another element that I want to discuss: I believe in miracles, and I believe that miracles happen when ordinary people do extraordinary things. I am a person with strong faith, and I believe that God is the center of my existence. I try, like many people, to figure out what role He actually plays in the process of our lives. Are we predestined or creatures of free will? Is His grace interactive or guaranteed by the promise of His love? It's not the premise of this book to enter into a deep theological discussion, but it's significant to note that these ideas fall under the category of mystery and faith, and mine is absolute.

Marianne Williamson comes close to helping me find my answer: "God doesn't work for us, He works through us." I think that means we're provided with the grace that allows miracles to happen if we have the courage—and now I am quoting my daughter from when we were skiing—to "just go for it."

So, there I was in my backyard surrounded by an eight-foot-high chain-link fence. Two little boys had moved into a house right on the other side. Every day I heard the sound of these kids playing baseball, calling each other Mike and Bill, and their voices made me believe they must be just about my age.

Okay, I thought, *the time is now.* I can even remember the date: May 10, 1956. All of the competitive anger that had been bubbling up inside a little blind boy galvanized in a moment of decision and action. I grabbed the chain link, pulling myself up hand-over-hand until I reached the top. A smart little guy would have grabbed the top of the fence and eased his way down the other side, but no, I was Tom Sullivan, daredevil. I leaped into space and crashed down on the hard New England ground, knocking the wind out of myself. The two little boys dropped their ball and gloves and came running over.

Billy Hannon, who has been my best friend for fifty years, looked down at this heap on the ground and said simply in his Boston accent, "Wow, that was a gnarly fall. I'm Billy Hannon."

"I'm Tom Sullivan," I croaked, "and I'm blind."

Billy's long "wow" was profound as he evaluated what he had just heard, and then he created my miracle. He said, with the beautiful innocence of a nine-year-old boy, "Want to play?"

With this invitation, Billy Hannon changed my life, and for the first time I had a friend who didn't care if I was blind or had two heads.

Though Billy Hannon was my first real friend, for a long time he was the only friend I had with two good eyes. Remember when you used to play games in the neighborhood and put your fingers out odd or even to decide who would be on a team? Well, every time the elected captains in my neighborhood played those pickup games I was always the last to be chosen; the one nobody really wanted. I remember hearing kids say, "Well, I guess you have to take him." So, I built up a tremendous level of frustration and, yes, even anger, that kept a chip on my shoulder for years until Patty kissed it away.

So many of the turning points that have been important in my life were brought about by Patty, and her absolute love and commitment. I suppose everybody hopes to fall in love. At least that's what the poets say. Certainly, I fell head-over-heels in love with Patty Steffen of Tucson, Arizona, but I was sure my blindness would be a major complication in our relationship. And

I wondered from early on whether it would be an obstacle to Patty's deciding to share her life with me.

I remember a conversation we had on the beach. I expected Patty to have all kinds of hesitation when I asked her to marry me in the moonlight. Patty not only wasn't hesitant, she got kind of angry when I began to mention potential problems.

Okay, I was down on one knee in the sand asking her to marry me, and before she had a chance to say yes or no I jumped up and went on stupidly, "And listen, I know it will be complicated, I mean, living your life with a blind person, but I know I can provide for us, and I think I can develop into a great father and husband, even though I'm sure you're gonna have to do all the driving. Hey, I could even learn to cook."

I thought I was being funny. She cut me off.

"Listen," she said—and this was the turning point—"your being blind is only part of who you are, Tom. I love you, not because you're blind but because you're you. I've waited for you all my life. I knew that the first night I heard you sing. You were meant for me. We're going to have a great life. And so, the answer is yes, yes, yes."

And she kissed me.

This was the first time anyone had made me understand that being blind was only part of who I was. At this turning point I learned another critical lesson, and it is that sometimes I need someone else—in this case, Patty—to provide me with the insight necessary to see life inside out.

Turning points can be as subtle as the gradual change in the seasons or as dramatic as one that happened to me on a June afternoon I will never forget.

Patty had gone to the store to shop for groceries. We had just moved from Boston to Beverly Hills, California, because I wanted to seek fame and fortune in the record business. At the time I was still carrying that chip on my shoulder. Patty had not quite been able to knock it off. The bottom line was I hadn't really grown up yet, even though I was married and had two children, three-and-a-half-year-old Blythe and year-and-a-half-old Tommy.

So, Patty had gone to the store, and my job was to watch the kids. The telephone rang, and when I picked it up I couldn't believe it. The guy on the other end was the talent coordinator for *The Tonight Show* starring Johnny Carson. Johnny and Ed McMahon had been out a couple of nights earlier having a few drinks in a night club where I was singing, and now I was being asked to do the show. My first big break in show business.

I was so involved in the conversation I never heard my little girl crossing the living room. I never heard the sliding glass door open or the sound of her feet on the deck. But I heard the sound of the splash when she fell in the pool.

I called her name. "Blythe!" I screamed, "Blythe!"

I ran outside, falling over chaise longues and other outdoor furniture, and eventually rolled into the swimming pool. I realized that the only way I could find my daughter was to dive down and grope along the bottom of the pool, hoping that I would touch her hand or her foot or anything.

Coming to the surface I screamed her name, counting the seconds. Twenty-one, twenty-two, twenty-three. Back down. I swam the length of the pool, praying I'd touch her, desperately praying I'd find her. Coming to the surface. Again. Forty-one, forty-two, forty-three.

For reasons I don't understand to this day I found myself standing in about shoulder-deep water, and I remember I looked up to heaven and said in anger, "God, I guess this is Your joke, isn't it? This child is going to die in this pool, and it's my fault because I'm blind. How can You let this happen?"

Another miracle.

"How can You let this happen?" I said again. And then I began to cry. And tears turned to prayers.

"Look, God," I bargained, "if You'll just give me our little girl back, I'll live an exemplary life. I'll make a difference to others."

As my tears mixed with the waters of the pool, I heard a quiet sound. It was the sound of her air bubbles, and they blip, blip, blipped their way to the surface. I followed them and dove down and found her in about nine feet of water, brought her up and respirated her. She is a remarkably healthy woman today.

In that microcosm of life, in that moment, at that turning point, I saw the best and the worst of what it was to be blind. The worst was that my child could have died in our swimming pool. The best was that I was able to find her because, as I just said, I heard her air bubbles.

You probably wouldn't hear air bubbles, not because you couldn't but because your sense of hearing probably isn't as developed as mine. And my hearing is developed this way only because I am blind.

So, there it is. A miracle. Inspired by God but provided through me. His gift but provided through me. It is in the context of the grace He offers all of us that I was able to save my daughter. It is through His Holy Spirit that my honest prayer for that miracle allowed a miracle to happen. Was it God being hands-on? That's the kind of theology argued by people of good faith, but what I'm sure about, what I'm absolutely convinced about, was that God heard my prayer. He always does.

> A miracle. Inspired by God but provided through me.

When I committed to living an exemplary life, I had no idea that it would lead to a life of real values and purpose. Over the years all of my books have been about improving the human condition and raising the nobility of the human spirit. I've given over three thousand lectures, working to convince people that the high road of morals and principles fits our best nature. In the world of nonprofits, I've been blessed to raise millions of dollars for causes that matter. And today, as I approach my senior years, I'm all about creating a legacy that shows I am committed to making a difference in the lives of others. Here's the wonderful secret to the performance of good works: you end up not only a better person but marvelously enriched each time you reach out to someone else. It's clearly the most rewarding philosophy to live by.

Making the most of your turning points requires you to be open to the experience. A turning point can be viewed as a positive or a negative. It all comes down to choice, and that choice goes beyond whether you're a glass-half-empty or a glass-half-full human being. The choice is about whether or not you believe that every experience is one of growth. Without these turning points there can be no expansion of who we are as people. Trial and, yes, tribulation are the critical negatives that provide us with the best options for our positives.

We also need enough self-confidence to believe that we're worthy of the goodness that God provides. More than any other element in my life, my turning points have provided me—and now you in these pages—with the best look I can offer into the process of living life inside out rather than outside in.

Consider your turning points a process of growth, even if they're formed through negative experiences. Remember that you can become a more fulfilled person just by evaluating them as opportunities for change. Think of it this way: only through an upward learning curve can we become our best selves.

At this stage of my life, in my seventh decade, I've come to understand that in God's wisdom—and through a faulty incubator—I came to this life as a blind child, but I'm now 100 percent convinced, through the process of my turning points, that my life as a blind person is far more useful to others than it would have been had I been able to see.

I mean it. I wouldn't have written all these books. I probably would not have been musical; I would have chosen sports over music as my vehicle of expression. I would have stayed in Boston and probably become a doctor or lawyer or some other kind of professional person, but I wouldn't have been given the opportunities that my blindness has presented.

> My life as a blind person is far more useful to others than it would have been had I been able to see.

So, here I am, writing you this text with a platform of, I hope, wisdom created through the process of turning points. Not a bad way to have spent a life. Thank goodness I'm only sixty-five, and there's plenty more time to continue to grow, think and, yes, love as God's instrument.

CHAPTER 7

Pride

IT WAS THE 1976 Super Bowl, held in Miami at the old Orange Bowl stadium. The Dallas Cowboys were preparing to play the Pittsburgh Steelers, and more important than the game it was America's bicentennial, our two hundredth birthday. I had been invited to sing the national anthem along with the international cast of Up with People—young men and women from over thirty countries who would join me on the field to pay tribute to our nation.

My emotions on that amazing afternoon were all over the place, but, frankly, as we prepared to walk to the center of the gridiron, the predominant feeling in my stomach was fear; absolute, unadulterated fear. When performers have sung our national anthem in recent Super Bowls the tracks were prerecorded, and in some cases even some of the performances themselves, allowing the singer to lip-sync. Back in 1976 there was no pretaping involved. I was going to walk out there and sing the national anthem with three hundred voices and no other accompaniment.

Rehearsal had gone very well, and up until about ten minutes before it was time to give my performance to the nation I was feeling fine. Then the fear set in. *What if I can't get the notes just right? What if my voice cracks? What if the sound system isn't perfect? What if the kids don't sing their parts correctly? What if . . . ? What if . . . ? What if . . . ?*

So, there we were, standing on the sidelines, and the announcer was saying, "Now, ladies and gentlemen, to honor America, the international cast of Up with People and Arista recording artist Tom Sullivan."

At that time Pete Rozelle was the commissioner of the National Football League. Rozelle was a good-sized guy, about six foot four, so when he walked up behind me on the sidelines and placed his hand on my shoulder, I could tell that the man was a dominant presence. He leaned close to me and said, "Young man, just remember, there are 90 million people listening to you sing this anthem, so don't mess it up."

That's all I needed: more panic.

Then there was the flyby. I think they were F-4 Phantom jets, but what I remember is that they passed low over the stadium, and the crowd roared. Something inside me connected the dots. The pride I felt in America—in a nation of freedom—swelled up in my chest. The sense that I was being asked to perform our national anthem, our statement of freedom, our commitment to free people all over the world, took away every bit of my fear.

Modestly, I must report that the day after our performance the *New York Times* said, "The Super Bowl game between the Cowboys and the Steelers was memorable but cannot compare to the national anthem performed by Up with People and blind recording artist Tom Sullivan."

Obviously that review inspired pride, which can have both

negative and constructive uses in our lives. In the concept of pride, there are inside-out elements that I think all of us need to understand. First, no one can establish personal pride without a positive self-image. What we think of ourselves is clearly what we project to others.

My transition from feeling disabled to joyously and remarkably able arose when I decided that being blind was the best thing that ever happened to me and that my perspective on life could offer others as much as I gained from them in return. When I came to believe that I had talents that other people could value, whether it was in sports, music, or publishing, I began to develop the self-image necessary to convey a sense of pride in every rela-

> Being blind was the best thing that ever happened to me.

tionship, in every goal I set, in every possibility of engagement with other human beings.

I'm constantly amazed when I meet people who are coping with adversity and yet take pride in achievement. Two years ago, the marvelous deaf actress, Marlee Matlin, performed on *Dancing with the Stars*, feeling the vibration of the music and experiencing the freedom of movement. The pride was obvious on her face. She also has often spoken of the idea that in a world of silence human beings can develop better concentration and a far greater awareness of people's visual signatures that say so much about who we are. When I spoke to Marlee, she told me directly that she was proud of being deaf as she works to change the picture that many people have of their fellow citizens who deal with hearing loss. Marlee is a prideful person for the right reasons.

A positive self-image allows a person to respect the self-worth of the other. We connect best when the lines of communications are clear, and that can most positively occur when two people find the synergism to feel good about themselves and even better about each other.

We often use the term *false pride*, and I think all of us would agree that we've seen it. It's created out of boastfulness, out of selling oneself too aggressively, out of someone's own insecurities that make them bombastic in their approach to a particular situation or other person.

Here's a personal favorite story. I was working for *Good Morning America* in the early eighties, and I was assigned to cover Mohammed Ali in his effort to regain the heavyweight championship of the world from Larry Holmes. The relationship between Holmes and Ali was really unique. Holmes had once been Ali's sparring partner at a time when Mohammed was the unrivaled best fighter on the planet. Larry Holmes respected Ali as only one gladiator can respect another gladiator.

If you are a boxing fan, you will remember how throughout the sixties and seventies Mohammed spouted the idea that he was "the greatest"—a claim he backed up with skills that had never been seen in the ring before or since.

I lived with the champ for ten days at his training camp, called Deer Lake, in Pennsylvania. We shared mornings doing a boxer's road work and nights with stories, music, and ice cream—Ali loved to eat it, even though it was breaking training.

I understood within the first few days he wasn't the same fighter he had once been. Boxing-induced Parkinson's was beginning to set in, and there were times when even punching the stationary bag seemed like an incredible effort for the champ. Yet Mohammed was still talking, pronouncing that he was the greatest whenever the press was around, telling them how he was going to take the title back from Holmes. False pride. Bravado. Runaway ego. Obviously, the champ was trying to build himself up, convincing himself to believe that there could be one more major comeback, that he could will his body to do it just one more time.

The fight was the saddest sports experience I had ever been a part of. Thankfully, the referee stopped it after eight rounds of pounding. The amazing thing was that the next day when we all looked at the tape, we saw that Larry Holmes never hit Ali in the face or the head. He just punished his body.

When I asked him about it, Holmes said, "Hey, listen, man, Mohammed is the greatest. I'm just a pretender. I didn't want to hurt him, you know? I love him."

Even in a brutal sport like boxing, a fighter can respect greatness when he sees it. Do you see where I'm headed? False pride is a curse to success. But I do think there is an antidote, the cure, the concept that has allowed me to overcome my blindness and avoid false pride. Try this acronym on for size: PRIDE is *Personal Responsibility for Individual Daily Effort*. In order to make pride work for us, we must take personal responsibility.

> False pride is a curse to success.

So often in the world of disability, I've seen friends cop out, blaming the disability for their failure, rather than taking personal responsibility for the way in which they are perceived and committing to a work ethic that allows them to succeed and grow. We sometimes have a bad habit of blaming the other guy for our own unwillingness to take that personal responsibility for our individual daily effort.

As with so many ideas in this book, good habits make up the foundation for turning our insight into external action. Nothing comes easy in any life, but when we achieve, based on our individual effort, when we establish an appropriate and committed work ethic, when we take responsibility for our actions and our circumstance, we become winners; and winning, my friend, is a habit. It arises out of a healthy pride we take in being special and being contributors to the world.

And about this idea of being special: when I developed the pride that allowed me to believe in myself and overcome a world of darkness, I also came to decide that my life needed to be the celebration of personal uniqueness. I figured out there wasn't anybody in the world who was quite like me, and since that was the case—to use a contemporary idea—I had something to market, something to sell. Being blind became a calling card, a marketing tool that has allowed me to find a wonderful place in the world. As long as I was willing to support my sense of pride with the habit of individual daily effort or hard work, I had the confidence necessary to try anything. I suppose that's why my career has been so varied.

> Being blind became a marketing tool that has allowed me to find a wonderful place in the world.

It was Roosevelt who said, "There is nothing to fear but fear itself," and fear arises from not knowing what's beyond our immediate purview. Confidence arises when inspiration and preparation come together in a habit of Personal Responsibility for Individual Daily Effort, or PRIDE.

Cleve McCleary is one of this country's most decorated Marines. During a combat mission in Vietnam, Cleve's squad was pinned down by heavy Vietcong fire. Through an act of unparalleled heroism, Cleve, though wounded, saved a number of his comrades, dragging them out of harm's way and guaranteeing their safety. In the process, he lost a leg and part of a hand. Despite his devastating injuries, Cleve went on to a wonderful marriage, a beautiful family, a life as a lecturer and writer, and a continuing commitment to the freedom he fought so bravely to protect. It was this gallant American who coined the acronym PRIDE as *Personal Responsibility for Individual Daily Effort,* and his life stands as a testimony to that commitment.

At sixty-five years old I understand that, like anyone, I'm affected by things that happen around me, things that happen outside my control. But if my own determinations are made from a place of insight that is inside out, life usually comes together, and the chances of accomplishing a positive outcome to any circumstance are virtually assured.

Please understand, I'm just as insecure as the next guy, but I do believe I found a formula in the acronym of PRIDE that serves as a mainstay, a foundation in the evolution of my character and my life.

CHAPTER 8

People

WHEN BARBRA STREISAND sang, "People who need people are the luckiest people in the world," she certainly could have been singing my song.

Clearly, my most significant insight is my awareness, and more importantly my gratitude to every person who has touched my life, expanded my point of view, and taught me something. In fact, this brings up a fundamental idea for really understanding life inside out.

Every life experience, every engagement with another human being, even if you believe that what you're going through is a negative experience, can turn out a positive result, even if that result seems to be a long way down the road.

Critics might hear me make this point and remind me that nations and, yes, people seem to carry on the same

> Every life experience can turn out a positive result.

behaviors over and over again. I suppose war is the ultimate example, but former enemies can prove to become great friends. Remember, the United States fought the British in the Revolution, yet over the centuries England has been our staunchest and most committed ally. Today we are terrific working partners with Japan and Germany, even though we fought a war that included the use of the first atomic bomb only sixty-seven years ago.

The never-ending study of each other represents, I believe, the never-ending search to find those elements in the other that create growth in ourselves; and that's why the game of people-watching—or in my case, people-listening—never seems to grow old.

I thought it might be instructive for me to talk about some of the people who have dynamically changed my life and what it was about them that allowed a blind person to see them clearly inside out and benefit from the uniqueness that made them special.

Marie and Thomas Sullivan, my mother and father. My father was a larger-than-life character. Though he was only five foot nine, his personality was that of Finn MacCooil, an Irish giant. Born in County Cork, my father immigrated to America as a little boy. Three weeks after the family arrived his father, my grandfather, died during the influenza epidemic, and my da was forced to leave school in the fourth grade and find a job to help support his mother.

He tried everything, but finally the luck of the Irish tapped him on the shoulder. Bootlegging expanded his business opportunities, and after a few years working for the Kennedy family running booze illegally up and down the New England coast, he made enough money to get into the pub business, also becoming one of Boston's most successful bookmakers— you know, the guys who take bets on sports. He also managed some pretty famous prizefighters, gambled, and read the racing forms the same way stockbrokers of the day studied the ticker tape.

Now, my father wasn't perfect. His marriage to my mother ended tragically in divorce. He was a functioning alcoholic, and his moods clearly qualified as Black Irish. But his impact on who I am today and how I see life cannot be denied. He was a grand storyteller, a shanicky who could take a half-truth and expand it into what he considered only an exaggeration. So, here I am, a writer.

Because part of his business was betting on sports, I've loved them from the day I could say Ted Williams. In his pubs he took great pleasure in entertaining. My first musical gigs included singing "Danny Boy" and other Irish ballads at a honky-tonk piano, and I suppose my fascination with show business occurred because of the people he introduced me to. I sang with the great Sophie Tucker, was hugged by Mae West, sat on Jimmy Durante's lap, and in later years met most of the stars of the day who came to play in one of my father's larger clubs.

I guess I was destined to be in the business, but Da's real contribution to my life was in his commitment to accessing me to the whole world. My mother and father saw things differently. For her, Tom needed to be smart, artistic, particularly musical, and committed to using his brains rather than brawn to find his place in the world. My father, on the other hand, was about manly things, and though I'm sure he was afraid as his son left the confines of the backyard, he took the risk. Looking back, they both struggled mightily to figure out what to do with me, and I wish today I could tell them they did a good job.

I remember he won an old thoroughbred racehorse in a poker game, brought it home in the middle of the night, tied it to our front door, and charged kids a nickel a ride, just to get children in the neighborhood to play with his blind son. He hung a buzzer on a basket in our driveway so Billy Hannon and I could shoot foul shots and play one-on-one. He made sure I saw at least twenty-five Red Sox games in Fenway Park every season and introduced me to all the players. At a Boston Celtics championship final in 1956 against the St. Louis Hawks we both got so excited in the third overtime that he spit his false teeth right out on the Boston Garden parquet floor, and we had to go down after the game and try to find them.

Everything my da did was built around his belief that his little boy had to take his place in the real world. Now, there was an oddity in his philosophy because my father could never use the word *blind*. He called me *sightless, handicapped, disabled, visually impaired*. Somehow he stated that he had a blind child. I don't know if it was a slight to his manhood or just his inability to accept imperfection, but that shadow, that haunting aspect, hung over our relationship until he died. In retrospect, it was my father who gave me the faith to believe that anything is possible if I was inventive and had—as he used to put it—real guts.

> My father gave me faith to believe that anything is possible if I was inventive and had real guts.

• • •

In every way, my mother filled in the other significant pieces in the making of Tom Sullivan, and in doing it she was a real taskmaster. Now, blind children have a habit of rocking back and forth or turning their heads from side to side and rubbing their eyes. I think much of this comes from our need to see life, as you do, with motion.

Friends have told me that sighted people are always looking at something, and so in a sense they are reassuring themselves that they are active and alive by observing the things that are going on around them. Blind people can do the same thing only by creating physical motion in themselves. My mother didn't allow any of that stuff to go on. Boy, how often I can remember her finger right in the middle of my chest to stop me from rocking, and if my head was turning back and forth she would embarrass me in front of people by asking me, "Thomas, who's winning the tennis game?"

Where my father had no real interest in my academic development, my mother would literally stand over my shoulder while I did my homework. And about music: though I wanted to play jazz and rock and roll she made sure I learned Beethoven, Bach, Brahms, and Chopin, along with some Rachmaninoff. Though her education was limited and her exposure to the world was not extraordinary, her desire for her son to be successful was, I believe, the central theme of her life. She was sure that the only way Tommy could find his place in the world was to be a little better at everything—a better singer, a better student, even a better athlete—and she believed that I needed to do that at the Perkins School for the Blind, the school that Helen Keller had attended. Boy, did they argue over that one.

My father wanted me in public school, probably because of his denial when it came to my disability. My mother was sure that I needed the involvement of special educators if I was ever going to succeed. The arguments they had night after night over me certainly must have been hard on my sisters, Jean and Peggy.

In the end I suppose both of them were right. The tragedy was that they couldn't share it together. My father and I ended up estranged. I hope we can find each other again in the next life. My mother died much too early. I so wish she could have had more time to enjoy my ride in show business, though I know she was proud of my early success.

Now, about my sisters. My sister Jean is fifteen years older than I am, so for me Jean was what I thought of as the treat sister. She was old enough to drive when I was little, so it was Jean who did all the nice things for me, or at least that's how I saw it. Because Jean married when I was eight years old and began to raise her own wonderful family, my relationship—and maybe this is a funny way to put it—was never made awkward by daily intimacy.

My sister Peg, on the other hand, was only eight years older than I was, so she bore the burden of having to be responsible for her little blind brother. In other books, I've written about how we tortured each other. I ruined Peggy's dating life because my mother made her take me with her on Saturday nights with her boyfriends. Because early on I loved the music of Ray Charles, Peggy convinced me that I was adopted and was actually black. Then there was the time she threw me in the ocean off the back of her boyfriend's boat and said that the sharks were out there. That's right: Jaws was going to eat me. I had a lot of nightmares over that one.

But then there were all the hours she worked with me on

term papers in high school, the talks we had as my mother and father's marriage broke apart, and her willingness to always pick me up at school. It's amazing for me to consider, looking back, that when I went to Perkins, a boarding school, it was Peggy or Jean who was always there either to take me to campus or to pick me up on weekends to take me home. I was so lucky to have had these sisters. Jean never missed filling in the space, making holidays like Thanksgiving and Christmas wonderful, even when our mother and father were fighting. When Jean had her own children I sort of became their big Uncle Tom and found an important family dynamic of love that I suppose had been missing.

I'm telling you all of this because of a fundamental truth. A family can be an amazing support system as you work to shake off the burden of a disability. Though my sisters acknowledged and supported those things that were necessary to keep a blind person upright and safe, they never made more out of my being blind than was necessary. Along with Billy Hannon, they set the tone for my childhood, and there are no words to thank them for the love they gave me.

Hank Santos, my piano teacher, was the finest overall musician I've ever had the chance to know and listen to—an African American whose musical range ran from winning major piano competitions in the classical field to being able to play great jazz. He really understood Tom Sullivan. When I would come in from my lessons, after about fifteen minutes of the classics, Hank would lean back in his chair, take a puff on his pipe, and say, "How about if we play a little Billie Holiday? Or maybe you could sing one of Ella's tunes."

This terrific teacher opened the door to everything that I

became in music. You see what I mean? Somebody has to find the button, tap into the possibilities that allow each of us to be special.

Hank had attended Boston University, where he shared a room with a rather famous American, Dr. Martin Luther King, Jr. My friend sensed my rage at being blind, my frustration at the labels and limitations people were placing on me. He exposed me early to Dr. King's writings and made me understand that the battle for equality would not be easy and would require me to be better than the people who tried to put me down.

Meeting Dr. King was a life-changing experience. He spoke to me about how I needed to channel my anger into goal-setting. He talked about my need to really get where people were coming from. By that he meant learning to define whether their prejudice arose from ignorance or malice. If it came from the former, I needed to become a teacher and in some ways turn the other cheek. If the prejudice came from malice or personal abuse, I needed to exercise my rights and speak up as a free citizen, knocking down the barriers and opening the doors to opportunities. Along with being the most important force in changing the social landscape of America, Dr. Martin Luther King, Jr. changed the life of a little blind boy.

Along with Hank Santos, another major influence on me when I was a student at Perkins was Tony Ackerman, my literature instructor. I just saw Tony recently. I think he's in his nineties now. He introduced me at a conference where I was the keynote speaker. He talked about the times he had graded my essays on the plays of Shakespeare and Eugene O'Neill that he had helped me to understand.

Then there were the conversations we had sitting outside under a tree at Perkins, sharing every subject under the sun. Tony Ackerman was my Mr. Chips—the person who brought literature and beauty into my life. Everything I am as a writer I owe to Tony Ackerman, and if my expression of ideas is clear it is because Tony made me understand the effective use of language as the ultimate gift of communication. Thank you, Tony. Thank you for giving me my literary voice.

My friend Billy Hannon comes up in a number of places in this book. Everyone needs a best friend, and when you have one you have to treasure him or her. At this writing Patty and I are preparing to go to the upcoming Super Bowl in Boston—not in Dallas where the game is really being played, but in Boston. We're looking forward to sitting in Billy's house, where we'll argue over the game, eat too much, and maybe even have a wee drop of Jameson Irish whiskey just to take off the New England chill.

Billy is my confidant, the male friend I talk to when I'm looking for good counsel, the person who never really considers my blindness but handles it automatically as if it is inconsequential to our relationship. I suppose that comes naturally from a little boy who simply said, "Want to play?"

Our game has been going on now for over fifty years, and I hope it will never end.

And then there's Betty White. Today Betty is everybody's Golden Girl, but for me she has been a friend, a mentor, a writing partner, and a person who in many ways became my surrogate mother when my own mother took her place with God in heaven. Betty and her husband, Allen Ludden, came to Cape Cod forty-three years ago, and serendipity brought us together.

Betty and Allen had come to do summer stock at the Cape Cod Playhouse. After performances they would show up at a little club called The Deacons' Perch where I was playing and singing. They would have a couple of drinks and maybe some clam chowder and ask me to perform some of their favorite songs. I remember they particularly enjoyed "Misty" and "Our Love Is Here to Stay."

On the other hand, what I was enjoying was the company of every good-looking lady who came into the club. And let me say—with a little bit of shame attached—I wasn't above using my blindness to get a date.

Before going on with this story, let me point out the inside-out cues that a blind person plugs into when assessing the pulchritudinous delights of the fairer sex. Most blond

> I wasn't above using my blindness to get a date.

girls have higher speaking voices, because they tend to originate in northern and central European countries. Dark-haired women carry the Latin huskiness of warmer climates and hotter blood. Women with great legs are always crossing and uncrossing them when sitting and also have longer strides when walking. Ladies who are voluptuous tend to be round-shouldered because they were embarrassed as young women, so their voices often seem to come from the center of their chests as a habit from girlhood. Women with long hair are always shaking their heads, and if you listen carefully, you can hear the rustle of beautiful tresses. And then there's eye contact; women who like their eyes send the sound of their voices along the same path because they're using their eyes as a vehicle to keep you focused in conversation. I probably shouldn't be giving these secrets away, but I suppose at sixty-five and being happily married for over forty years I don't need them anymore.

So, back to the story.

One night a rather attractive miss asked me to sing the recent hit, "By the Time I Get to Phoenix." When the song was finished she asked with a tear in her eye, "Listen, do you mind telling me something?"

"No," I said. "Anything."

"Do you mind if I inquire how you became blind?"

So, here I go with an "expansion" of stories like my father.

"Oh," I said, "I was an F-4 pilot in Vietnam. I was shot down and then spent some years in Haiphong prison, and you're the first beautiful girl who's spoken to me since I came home."

May I say here, in telling this story, I offer every person who has served this nation an apology for my insensitivity.

That was enough for Betty White and Allen Ludden.

"Tom," Betty said, "you're full of crap, and you are missing something wonderful. There's a girl who comes in here every night and sits alone at a front table. If you could see her eyes as she listens to you sing and watches you, I don't think you'd be dating anyone else. Call it an instinct or an insight, but I know I'm right. Now, come with me." She took my arm and led me to a table in front of the stage. "Excuse me," she said to a young woman sitting there. "This is Tom Sullivan, and your name is?"

"I'm Patty Steffen," she said shyly.

"Sit down here, Tom," Betty commanded. "I think this is where you belong."

Boy, was she right. That was Patty, and we've been married for all these years.

Allen Ludden went on to provide me with my first opportunities in show business. There was a shot on *The Mike Douglas Show*, and then he invited me to California, where he introduced me to record company executives, managers, and agents. I owe my career to Allen Ludden and Betty White, but there has been so much more to our relationship.

My first guide dog, a beautiful golden retriever named Dinah, retired and went to live with Betty after the death of her husband. As our relationship grew even closer, we collaborated on three books, *The Leading Lady*, *Dinah's Story*, and a recent novel entitled *Together*. We have both served as president of the Morris Animal Foundation, the largest funder of health studies for dogs, cats, horses, and wildlife in the world. She is truly the grandmother to our two children, Blythe and Tom, and has even come skiing with us in Colorado. That's right; there's nothing our Golden Girl won't do, and there's nothing that I don't share with this most special person.

No one had more of an effect on my professional life than Michael Landon. Michael and I became friends during his days on *Little House on the Prairie*, and I had the chance to write music, scripts, and even perform with him on episodes of *Highway to Heaven*.

Michael taught me the courage of conviction. Whenever we worked on a script and I would worry about whether the audience would get what I was trying to say, Michael would say, "Listen, Tom, just tell it like it is." He meant don't be afraid, don't back off, be as honest as you need to be. Don't just give the people what they want, make them think. Challenge their values.

He was also the guy who knew more great jokes and stories than anyone I've ever met, and once he even left the set and let a blind guy direct the last three scenes of the day.

I asked him once, "Why did you let me do that?"

"Because someday," he said, smiling, "you'll be the first blind person to succeed at it."

> "Someday, you'll be the first blind person to succeed at it."

Michael was the single most open creative artist I've ever known. You could try anything with Michael as long as you showed up prepared, knew your lines, were on time, and brought energy to the set. Discipline and values—that's what I got from Michael Landon, and also a dose of celebrity reality.

One night when the Red Sox were playing in the World Series, a bunch of us went to a bar to have some burgers, beer, and play pool. Boy, was that fun. And I got pretty loud.

A guy in the bar walked up and tapped me on the shoulder.

"You're Tom Sullivan," he said.

"Yeah, that's right," I said.

"Well, you know what, I have a little blind child, and watching you in here tonight I think you're a jerk."

Wow. I was rocked back on my heels. Honestly, my behavior was not out of line, but Michael summed it up.

"Listen, Tom," he said, "in the privacy of your own home you can do whatever you want, but if you're going to take their money and be a star, when you step out into the public you belong to them, and you better remember it."

Major lessons for an up-and-coming performer. Betty White, Allen Ludden, and Michael Landon taught me to be a professional, and they taught me to have the insight to understand what it truly meant.

From my friend Jack Nicklaus I learned priorities. I don't think he actually taught me very much golf. In fact, when I asked Jack what he thought of my golf swing when we were working on a story for *Good Morning America*, he said, "Well, Tom, the best thing I can say about your swing is that you don't ever have to see it."

Okay, Jack, it's ugly, I know it! What Jack really taught me has very little to do with the lessons I got on the golf course; it had to do with my sense of values. When I asked the greatest golfer in history how he prioritized his life, he said quickly, with absolutely no hesitation, "Tom, my family always comes first, my golf comes second, and, well, my business comes third."

When I receive his Christmas card every year and Patty describes his children, their spouses, and enough grandchildren to put together a couple of baseball teams, I realize that Jack has really lived by those principles, and though I haven't spent as much time as I'd like to with Jack and his beautiful wife, Barbara, I get the sense that she has been his rock, much as Patty has been mine.

And so, we come to Patty. How to describe my wife? And how to explain what she has meant to my growing inside out?

I will never see the Northern Star at night, but if the phrase *constant as the Northern Star* has validity, that's how Patty has loved me—constant, never failing, never doubting.

This Christmas I gave her a small heart on a silver chain engraved on the back with a message, "My heart is always with you." When you give yourself to someone so completely as Patty and I have over all these years, the bond is unbreakable.

In a marriage, when it really works, there's the you person, the me person, and then the us person—an entity, a place from where Patty and I make all of our decisions. From here we draw our strength as two people who are always on the same page, sharing as one, committed to a common purpose in the raising of our children

Patty is my eyes on the world, and I like to think that in that way I'm not really blind.

and in the operation of our lives, and most important in the love and joy that we share through our intimacy. We are one, and Patty is my eyes on the world, and I like to think that in that way I'm not really blind.

For a short time, Patty had considered a life as a nun. She even spent a few months in a convent examining the possibility of taking her vows. I am convinced that God sent her here just for me.

Our children, Blythe and Tom, are certainly our most important creations. For the most part we have lived a charmed life as a family. Oh, sure, there have been plenty of bumps along the way and even some pain, but I believe we have been a very successful family unit. What you hope for is that when your kids grow up you can become good friends, and that has happened for the Sullivans.

Tom and I have made a lot of music together. He's a terrific bass player, songwriter, producer, and recording engineer. We also play plenty of golf and enjoy the ocean together on paddleboards.

Blythe is my ski guide, movie critic, party planner, clothing consultant, and most importantly, a football fan—naturally, the New England Patriots. These two great people are human beings I not only love because they're my children, but I have come to like and admire them because they're special. What a great thing for a dad to be able to say.

The most significant thing they've taught me is how to adapt. I really wondered whether I could be a successful parent, being blind. My children, out of pure love, taught me that all I really had to do was to learn to operate under a different set of rules. I could coach Tom's baseball games. I could talk to Blythe about the horseback riding she loves and even get on one myself. We could share music, and I was pretty good at helping with their homework. Being able to adapt to a circumstance is a critical necessity if you're ever going to grow. Though I've noted that concept in other parts of this book, the connection between a blind parent raising kids in a sighted world and growing in the experience makes my children crucial people in my life and teaches me that through others we can become far more fulfilled. There's an interplay of ideas that runs concurrent in these pages. It's an overlap brought about through the engagement in relationships in a way that's central to life as I see it.

Now, I'm sure there are a lot of you who would disagree with me when I make this statement: without spirituality in your life you're just not whole. I mean it. I don't think you're a complete person—or maybe it's better to say a balanced human being—

> Without spirituality
> in your life you're
> just not whole.

without God as part of your life.

I didn't always understand this idea, but it has been made very clear to me through my relationship with my friend the Reverend Clayton Cobb. Clayton is a Presbyterian minister, the pastor of St. Peter's by the Sea Presbyterian Church in Rancho Palos Verdes, California. He's also my running partner when I don't run with my guide dog.

Cobb has brought focus to my spiritual journey and made it possible for me to make my faith the underpinnings of my whole life.

For my recent novel, *A Short Life Well Lived*, Clayton served as a sounding board during our morning runs, arguing every point of spirituality and theology. We discussed everything from the existence of God to the roles He plays in our lives. Oh, these were incredible discussions, and often they became rather heated when we talked about God as an active participant or when we argued about the role of grace and free will, and who really gets to go to heaven, and what the true consequence of sin is, and most importantly, God as the absolute force of total love.

Clayton is beautifully spiritual and a great communicator, along with being a person who backs it up with a spectacular intellect. His church is fortunate to have him but no more fortunate than I am to call him my friend.

There are so many other people who have influenced my life, but I've written these short profiles to make a point that I consider critical in my own evolution as a person. People do need people, and we need to approach each other with open hearts and minds.

In the introduction to this text I wrote that I have never met a person who was ugly unless they wanted to be, unless what they expressed was ugliness; and I'm convinced that's the case. People's behavior toward one another can be self-absorbed and even cruel. It arises out of a false assumption that what they want out of the situation or circumstance is all that matters. For anyone who thinks that way, the phrase "we reap what we sow" couldn't be more accurate.

The important insight in this chapter relates back to my conversation on interdependence. As I noted, we are all interdependent, but that's only the practical side of our relationship to people. Barbra has it right. People do need people, and when we appreciate each other, we understand we are truly the luckiest people in the world. And where is it that we

> When we appreciate each other, we understand we are truly the luckiest people in the world.

find the elements that connect us? Well, okay, a hug or a handshake feels good. A slap on the back in fellowship connects us. But it's the insight we gain through intimate conversation, trust, and willingness to show our own vulnerability that humanizes us and provides us with the insight necessary to find the balance we share one with another.

The person who has influenced me more than any other in the course of my life's journey was only eleven years old. She wasn't famous. None of you would know her. Her achievements were not remarkable, except to me. But there isn't a day when I don't remember my friend Molly.

About twenty-five years ago ABC's *Good Morning America* sent me to Winter Park, Colorado, to profile a remarkable group of kids and volunteer adults who came there from MD Anderson Cancer Center in Houston, Texas. The idea was that these children who were struggling with this dreaded disease would have the opportunity to enjoy a winter and skiing experience in Colorado.

To say the Sullivan family got involved with these special kids would be an understatement. Both my son, Tom, and my daughter, Blythe, learned to work as instructors in the program. Tom even developed the ability to ski on one ski with outriggers, just like the amputee kids; and I spent my evenings playing the piano, singing, and telling stories, while Patty worked as kind of a housemother, making sure all the kids were tucked in safely at the end of every busy day.

What I can still feel, thinking back on that experience, are the hugs from these special children. Hugs can say a lot, and there was a lot being said every day we were in the mountains.

Over the next three years, the Sullivans chose to join our special friends outside of my professional responsibility, principally due to my most inspirational person—eleven-year-old Molly Newbury. When I first met Molly she had just begun her treatment, and even though back then chemo was tougher than it is now, Molly's ebullient spirit was palpable and undeniable. She loved being in the snow. She loved sharing with her friends. And I think she fell in love with the Sullivan family and most particularly Dinah, my golden retriever guide dog.

There were some nights when Dinah would sleep with Molly

rather than with us. It was almost as if the big golden retriever understood that Molly needed the love she provided more than we did. Animals are like that, you know. I see it all the time with the dogs I work with. Anyway, we all fell in love.

In the second year Molly had lost a leg to the disease, but it sure didn't stop her. She spent her ten days working with our son, and by the end she was flying down the mountain as an amputee. In the third year, though she was very sick, Molly still returned for the winter vacation. This time, the doctors had removed her other leg. I just couldn't believe her spirit.

"So, I can't ski," she told me. "I guess I'll just have to go down the mountain in a sled."

And that's what she did, laughing all the way.

On the last night we were together the program held a dance for all of the kids and the volunteers. I was sitting with Molly on the sidelines because I'm a lousy dancer and, well, because Molly couldn't dance. Boy, was I wrong.

"Pick me up, Tom," she said, "I want to dance."

"Hey, Molly," I protested, "I'm not much of a dancer."

"Don't worry about it," she said in her thick Texas accent. "I'll tell you where to go so we don't knock anybody over."

I picked her up, and we waltzed and sashayed around the room. And as far as I was concerned we were Fred Astaire and Ginger Rogers. It was a moment I'll never forget.

Back in our chairs I heard Molly sigh, and I asked her how she was feeling.

"I'm pretty tired," she said. She paused. "I'm really tired."

"Are you sleeping okay?" I asked.

"Yeah," she told me, "and last night I had a dream. A really special one."

"Oh?" I asked. "What did you dream about?"

Her response has stayed with me every day of my life and in many ways is the underpinning of my own faith.

"I dreamed that
the angels came."

"I dreamed that the angels came," she said simply.

I choked back a tear and asked, "Well, what did they say, Molly?"

Her answer was so childlike and yet so profound.

"They told me they'd take care of me and that I'd get to see them pretty soon."

I am convinced that Molly Newbury sees the angels every moment of eternity. I'm sure that she's with them in heaven, and even more I believe quite likely she has become one of them. The cherubim and seraphim are very lucky to have her, and maybe in God's plan Molly was always meant to join the heavenly host.

When I think of my friend Molly Newbury I'm consoled by the idea that I'm working every day to be a good enough man so that someday I'll join her, and maybe we'll ski another mountain. Then Molly will have both of her legs, and I'll be able to see.

Anyway, that's what I'm hoping for.

Thank you, Molly, for being the most inspirational person in my life.

CHAPTER 9

Purpose

WHEN A MAJOR corporation writes a mission statement, it's defining its purpose, its reason for being. The statement is their declaration that this is who they are.

Every successful person I have been blessed to know—and by *successful* I mean balanced as a human being—has been purposeful. On the other hand, I've known some terrific people who would agree that they have been lost on their life journey. Why? Because they never found that true purpose, their life compass.

It wasn't until my experience in Rome, noted in the prologue of this book, that I understood life inside out, and the possibilities for applications of this principle opened up and took shape. Here's a confession I've never made before, either in other books or in public interviews. I think I found my real purpose—and understood my purpose—when I was about fifty years old. (This is a different experience than the one I described in the prologue.) That may seem odd to those of you who know anything about me because certainly I've had a wonderful life, but my

> I found my real purpose when I was about fifty years old.

motivations over the first fifty years were segmented into each specific thing I was doing at the time. For example, when I wanted to make it on the wrestling team during high school, I gave it everything I had in practice or in matches.

In the same way, I worked very hard when I decided that I would apply myself and study so that I could go to Harvard. Certainly you could say that I was often purposeful in my intent, but these were immediate kinds of goals that I was setting, some of them short-term and some of them moderately long-term. There was no overriding philosophy attached to my actions. The experience with Michelangelo's sculptures framed the way in which I see my life inside out. So, when I talk about the corporations that create a mission statement I'm discussing a much deeper and broader intention. The kind of purpose I'm referring to begins for all of us with a dream, expressed consciously or felt subconsciously. It takes shape when that dream grows into a belief and then becomes an action that leads to a result.

Say it this way—if you can dream it, see it clearly, believe in it, you can absolutely achieve it; you can become purposeful as a person. The difference between setting goals and being a truly purposeful human being has to do with a critical piece of insight: How do you see yourself? Who are you at your core? And do you have a balance between the ultimate idea of purpose and the reality checks that are necessary to keep us on track? Listen, I know I'm not going to be shooting hoops with the L.A. Lakers in the NBA, but if I work hard enough at it in my backyard, I can beat my son in a free-throw contest with a buzzer attached to the basket. It's critical that in determining a purpose you reach higher than your actual grasp, understanding you might come up a little short.

> It's critical that in determining a purpose you reach higher than your actual grasp.

When I think of my wife, Patty, I understand that she has unlimited capabilities and interests. She's a successful Realtor, helping people find just that right home. She's active in community, raising money for a number of important causes. She cares about staying fit and watching her diet. But if you ask her, she will say without hesitation that her most important purpose—the element that makes her purposeful—is her essential role as wife and mother. If Patty wrote her mission statement it would read: My mission is to be the best wife and friend to my husband, Tom, and mother to my children—Blythe and Tom.

So, I became a purposeful person, a guy who discovered my purpose, when I realized—as I mentioned earlier—that being blind was the best thing that ever happened to me, but this realization came in what was seemingly an incongruous moment.

The ballroom of the New York Marriott was full. A number of the city's most influential people, along with my family and friends, had put on formal wear and come to celebrate the American Foundation for the Blind Helen Keller Achievement Award, given only twice in the eighty-year history of the organization. As I stood under the glow of the spotlight and listened to the master of ceremonies wax eloquently over my accomplishments, I found myself wondering. What had I done that was truly special or remarkable? Had I really made a difference in the lives of others, or had I been just an anomaly, an oddity to those with sight, a blind person who had lived his life as a risk-taker? Was I blind first or a person who happened to be blind?

I was fifty years old, and it seemed odd to be asking these questions, but I suppose we all arrive at crossroads of reflection, and if we're going to grow these moments are necessary.

I understood that at my core I wanted—no, needed—to be a contributor to the common good. Were my achievements tangible enough to serve a purpose, or did they just make for good press? Who benefited because I could hit a golf ball well or ski fast, run marathons, or even sing well? My writings have been principally about me, and here I go again. Had I said anything that was more than just a sound bite?

Balancing the life scale, I knew I'd been a good father and husband. I believed I was a friend others could count on, and looking back under the glare of that spotlight I was comfortable in the knowledge that for the most part I had followed the old rule and treated others the way I wanted to be treated. Fine, but what would be my legacy? How would people benefit from the fact that I had been here?

> At my core I wanted—no, needed—to be a contributor to the common good.

At that moment on the stage in front of three thousand well-dressed and well-heeled patrons, it dawned on me that my life needed to be about ideas. My legacy would be measured by my ability to articulate my perceptions into life lessons that would be tangible to others. What were the real life lessons that could be drawn from a life without sight?

So, as I stood on the stage I felt my pulse quicken with an excitement unlike I'd ever known. For the first time, I understood that my circumstance—the blindness that to others was a handicap, a life burden, a weight often pushing them down—was for me a circumstance that had presented me with the opportunity to contribute to others and truly make a difference. If I could be the best Tom Sullivan possible, who happened to be blind, and that blindness served a significant purpose to others by motivating them or touching their lives in ways I might not immediately understand, how could I not feel wonderful about it?

Here I was, being honored with an award named after arguably the single most remarkable person history has ever produced. No one had ever achieved to the level of Helen Keller against the odds of adversity so large, so daunting that it was almost impossible for me to grasp the scope of her accomplishments. And now here I was with the master of ceremonies suggesting that I belonged in the same rarified air of achievement.

Let me say right here and now that anything I've done with my life pales in comparison to Ms. Keller's accomplishments. But the award served as my personal wake-up call to purpose and committed me to a decision that has been my constant—my mission statement:

*I will live my life as a person of good purpose, one
who is committed to making a difference and being
purposeful in the pursuit of excellence.*

What I've just described is rather dramatic, I know. It has the feeling of some higher power reaching down, tapping me on the head, and saying: *Okay, it's time for you to step up, Sullivan. It's time for you to do something with your life.* Honestly, I'm not trying to overamplify my situation; it's just that my calling happened that night on the stage, and I do believe in callings.

My friend Clayton Cobb, the pastor I've talked about, tells me that his calling occurred while he was receiving Communion at a Sunday service. He described the feeling as the arrival of the Holy Spirit, touching his heart and lifting his soul—filling his being with an overwhelming, abundant sense of purpose.

Again, dramatic, but you hear about this kind of purposeful impact in many walks of life. I've heard people say, "I always knew I wanted to be a doctor," or in the case of my colleagues in show business, "I never had any doubt about wanting to be an actress." It helps when your purpose is very clear-cut.

My son, Tom, has recently opened an exciting new business designing and manufacturing surfboards. Surfing is something he's loved from the time he was ten years old. He has traveled all over the world, chasing the big waves, and for him surfing has been a life passion. And now he has found a way to blend this love of the sport and the ocean with a purposeful endeavor working to build a successful business.

Here's the one proof I'm sure of: finding purpose, writing your mission statement, and becoming a purposeful person may be hard to execute but is always definite. By that I mean that when your purpose is staring you in the face, the feeling, the vibe, the buzz is absolutely clear. We get it. People just *know* when they've discovered their purpose.

> People just *know* when they've discovered their purpose.

So, my insight for this chapter is simple. Keep searching. Don't give up. Failure or redirection doesn't have to be a negative experience. Taking risk, trying something new, reaching for the gold are all learning experiences that in the end will serve you well in pursuing your purpose. If at times you feel aimless and lost, rudderless without a sense or commitment to a purpose, don't worry. We're all in the same boat. As Pollyanna as this may sound, I believe every human being who lives on our blue ball spinning through space was designed by the Creator to have a purpose, to be valuable, to count for something.

CHAPTER 10

Passion

PASSION. IT'S MY favorite word, and it's the single most important ingredient that allows all of us to see life inside out rather than outside in.

The reason for this is quite simple. Passion arises out of the beating of our hearts, the yearning of our souls, the intensity of our desires, the confidence that allows us to risk failure in order to gain success. Living from our passion is the very essence of living life from the inside out.

Long before I understood the meaning of the word, passion was the necessary energy I needed to break out of the world of darkness and enter a world full of light.

> Passion was the necessary energy I needed to break out of the world of darkness.

As a kid, I was passionate about the Red Sox, never missing a game on the radio and knowing all the players' batting averages, how many home runs they hit, and how many games the Sox won in a season. I was a walking baseball card, a six-year-old statistician with all the figures in my head, but that was being passionate about something, rather than having a passion that prompted a substantial action.

My first active passion was music, and the first song I can ever remember singing in front of anyone wasn't just one tune; it was all the Irish ballads that my father played on our old Victrola, and I copied them note for note.

John McCormack was the great Irish tenor my father listened to night after night, and by the age of five I could sing everything from "Danny Boy" to "Galway Bay," from "Too-Ra-Loo-Ra-Loo-Ral" to "When Irish Eyes Are Smiling," and even raucous bar tunes like "Steve O'Donnell's Wake" and "The Wild Colonial Boy" and my father's evening favorite when he was in his cups, "Dear Old Girl." I admit it: I loved standing in our living room singing for my da's cronies, and the first time I made them cry crooning "Danny Boy," I knew I was passionate about music and musical expression.

The Irish songs were not the only tunes I warbled early on. There were country songs like Hank Williams's "Hey Good Lookin'" and "Your Cheatin' Heart," and rock and roll like "Blueberry Hill" and "Tutti Frutti" from Little Richard and Fats Domino. There was no question that my passion, turned into musical action, has served me well over all these years.

And then there was my passion for books. I was a voracious reader, preferring talking books for the blind to reading in Braille. I loved the voices of some of the readers who gave their time on behalf of blind people, sharing their talents and bringing the classics to life. My favorite of those readers was Alexander Scourby, an English actor with a voice as melodious as that of Richard Burton. Works like *Ben-Hur*, *The Last Days of Pompeii*, *Treasure Island*, and *A Tale of Two Cities* came to life on the first LP-sized discs that played 33 ⅓ rpms on the talking book machine given to me by the Perkins School for the Blind.

Wrestling became a sport that provided the physical outlet I needed for my passions, and I'll have more to say about that in other pages.

Where I'm going with all this—what I'm trying to bring forward in this chapter—is the idea that passions translated into actions allow us to grow, to experience life, to never have to live on the sidelines but be fully and completely engaged in the game; and for a blind child that idea was critical. It started for me with dreams and imagination, clearly ideas that establish themselves inside out, and once the concepts had taken shape, I directed them through my passion into action.

Obviously, there are other passions in my life. Certainly, my wife and children are at the top of the list. And then there are small ones—cheeseburgers with grilled onions, coffee milkshakes, and then, frankly, the Irish curse—a wee draft of Irish whiskey on the rocks.

A celebration of passion is, I believe, the celebration of life; and the point was made crystal clear to me when I was given the opportunity to spend time with Dr. Viktor Frankl. If I

> A celebration of passion is, I believe, the celebration of life.

were on a desert island and had only one book to read outside of the Bible, it would be Dr. Frankl's classic, *Man's Search for Meaning.*

Pre–World War II was the golden age of clinical thinking in

Vienna. Freud, Adler, Jung, and Dr. Frankl were the four great psychiatrists probing the human psyche for answers, working to learn the mystery and complexity of the human mind.

At the onset of World War II, Dr. Frankl and his family, along with millions of other Jews, were confined to concentration camps by the Nazis. It is impossible for any writer to articulate the horror of those circumstances unless they'd been there. To survive, Dr. Frankl imagined beauty. He willed his mind to picture snow falling on the trees, a winter scene of idyllic joy; and somehow, some way he survived. Out of this experience he evolved his logotherapy, an approach to clinical patient care that deals with the now, the place you're in, the reality of your human experience, and your purpose in life as its most essential meaning and drive.

I met him in the late seventies when I had just completed my first book with my friend, author Derek Gill. Derek was preparing to write a Frankl biography, and the remarkable Austrian, along with his second wife, had come to stay with the Gills for a few days in Palos Verdes, California. I was invited to a luncheon to meet the great man. He had been given a copy of *If You Could See What I Hear*, the biography that Derek and I had written, and he surprised me with his enthusiasm for the work.

Pounding the table and shocking us all, the elderly gentleman said in his heavy accent, "Tom, you represent everything I believe, and do you know why?"

"No," I stammered, having absolutely no idea what he might be getting at.

"You," he said, "like me, are a survivor. You had taken the adversity of your disability and turned it into a positive. And do you know how you have done that?"

Stunned, I waited for him to go on.

"Young man, you have done that," he said, "by exercising your passion."

He placed a half-full glass of water in my hand.

"You see," he said, "you are a glass-half-full human being, and that is because you are willing to believe in the unlimited capacity of human passion."

I think I may have said *amen* to the end of this pronouncement. I was rocked and humbled that this man, who had endured so much, believed that I could add value to the world at large. I was only thirty-one or thirty-two and certainly did not have the seasoning to trust the balance of my own personality. At that time I was still struggling to understand my place in the world and certainly had not cultivated an inside-out view of life, but I think that what Dr. Frankl saw in me was the potential to be an instrument of change, to be valuable, and to express all of my hopes, dreams, and aspirations through the applications of my passions.

> "You are willing to believe in the unlimited capacity of human passion."

I believe it's our passion that provides us with the courage to take risks. Without our passion I'm convinced that our fears will overwhelm us and hold us down.

Now, I suppose that there are people who would say that I've engaged my passions to a fault, and if you ask my family, they would say that some of my flights of fancy have been . . . well, extreme. In sports it's been marathons and triathlons and working to master the great game of golf. Oh, yeah, and then there's skiing with Blythe and some bungee jumping in New Zealand just for fun.

In music, my performances have ranged from traditional choral works like the *Messiah* to performing pop music and jazz around the world. My passion as an advocate for the disabled has placed me on presidents' councils, along with lobbying Congress in the eighties for the passage of the ADA (Americans with Disabilities Act) and other important pieces of legislation, along with all the books, like this one, that I've had the pleasure of writing, advocating the positive and unlimited potential of those of us with the inconvenience of a handicap.

When you operate from a place of passion, even the smallest things can matter. I actually look forward to a cheeseburger with everything smothered on it from In-N-Out, a fast food restaurant in Southern California where the burgers are simply divine; and, as you already know, I have a bad habit of enjoying a dram of wonderful Irish whiskey; and then there's the occasional Cuban cigar.

I'll bet you grasp my meaning. Once you get your passions to flow, life becomes worth living and achievement of your goals seems always within your reach.

Once you get your passions to flow, life becomes worth living and achievement of your goals seems always within your reach.

I love senior citizens who clearly never really grow old because they're buoyed up by their passions. Recently, Betty White sent me a calendar of her schedule for a particular month, and I realized—to my shock—that I would not have the energy to cope with the number of things she had to achieve.

I said, "Listen, how do you expect to get all of this stuff done?"

"Oh," she said, smiling, showing her famous dimples, "when you're my age you don't have to sleep very much. There's always time."

And there's always passion. Betty loves her craft; she loves her life.

So did George Burns. I met him when he was in his nineties at a party thrown by some Beverly Hills friends. It was the night that Groucho Marx died, and Mr. Burns was asked by the press to comment on his relationship with Groucho. He said all the right things, but then, in a quiet moment while puffing on his cigar, he said, "I don't want to talk about the past, kid. I'm living in the present and thinking about the future."

Then there was Jack LaLanne, who recently passed away at age ninety-six. I met him when he was about ninety, and it was embarrassing in the middle of the Beverly Hills Hotel when he challenged me to a contest doing one-armed push-ups. Let me say, it was no contest. He creamed me, both left- and right-handed.

And then there's Joe Norwood. Mr. Norwood was still teaching ten to fifteen golf lessons a week at age one hundred and was considered one of America's finest instructors. His stories about Bobby Jones, Ben Hogan, Sam Snead, and others made taking a golf lesson far more important than just learning to hit a five iron.

These stories are meant to be illustrations of my critical point. The passions expressed by some remarkable people who have lived on the planet a long time make aging just a number. Their passions lift them, buoy them up, make every day worthwhile and allow us to treasure them for years to come.

The other thing about the expression of our passions that

really is an inside-out life secret is an idea that I completely embrace. The expression of our passions creates the habit of being a passionate person, and that's a label I'm delighted to accept. It puts me in great company: I intend to be Betty White, George Burns, Jack LaLanne, and Joe Norwood—growing old gracefully but as a passionate human being.

CHAPTER 11

Turning Disadvantage into Advantage

EVERY SINGLE DISADVANTAGE in life can be turned into an advantage. I want to say it again: every single disadvantage in life can be turned into an advantage, without exception, and I believe in this concept with absolute certainty.

Why? you might ask. Why do I feel this way? Why am I so sure? Because my life has been a laboratory of proving it. Because in order to overcome the darkness of blindness I had to build my life around this singular belief. It arose out of trial and error. It manifested out of my own insecurity. It had a number of starts and stops when I doubted and my faith wasn't as strong. But at this stage of my life I am as confident in this idea as it's possible to be.

Let's begin with the loneliness of my childhood. I've already written about the fenced-in backyard and the fact that I spent years listening to the world outside and wanting to be part of it. The compensation was in my absorption with radio dramas: listening to them, hearing the language. Learning plot structure and character development turned my own imagination loose and helped me to grow and become a writer.

So, here I am, fourteen books later. Movies, TV series, music, and poetry—I've tried them all. And all of this joy rose out of the loneliness and confinement of my fenced-in yard. Even my friendship with Billy Hannon found its beginning in my need to break out of the prison, to climb the fence, to be angry enough to take a risk. When he said, "Wanna play?" it became the mantra for the rest of my childhood (i.e., disadvantage to advantage).

So, sports and music became my tickets out of darkness, and the sport I picked to participate in against sighted athletes was wrestling. Let me say unequivocally, in the beginning I was horrible. I lost the first fifteen matches in two minutes and twenty-three seconds altogether. I was so bad I didn't even have a chance to get the uniform dirty. The coach we had at the time was a rather cynical guy, and I remember going out for the sixteenth match, hearing him say, "Listen, Sullivan, the kid you're going to compete against is a much better athlete than you are, so just go out there and try not to embarrass me, okay?"

Okay, I thought. *If it's that bad, why worry?* And when I began to relax I performed much better. Sure, I lost that match, but I went on to win championships all over the world and actually am fortunate to be a member now of the Wrestling Hall of Fame.

So, where's the disadvantage-to-advantage part? Well, I was competing against a kid from the Soviet Union. The score was 11 to 3. The Russian was ahead. Every time he knocked me down it became more painful. Now, I happen to have plastic—that's prosthetic—eyes. My real eyes were lost to glaucoma.

With plastic eyes you take them out at night and wash them off and then put them back in. The next time the Russian knocked me down, I just reached up and popped out one of the little devils and dropped it on the mat.

"Stop, stop," I said.

"Why?" he said in Russian.

And then he looked down and saw the eye. And, well, that was too much for his stomach. He threw up all over the mat. Somewhere out there in the record books it says *Sullivan over Asmanoff by default*. Now, that's turning disadvantage into advantage.

So, whether it's in sports, education, disability, family relationships, or any other person-to-person involvement, the record is replete with stories of human beings who have taken adversity by the neck, given it a shake, and turned it into advantage. Believe me when I tell you that the formula is foolproof if you just give it a try.

The record is replete with stories of human beings who have taken adversity by the neck and turned it into advantage.

Here's a fact: the process of turning disadvantage into advantage can't effectively occur without engaging others.

I ride my tandem bike with a special friend, veterinarian Dr. Robert Hilsenroth, the former director of the Morris Animal Foundation, an organization I've supported for years. I've had the same running partners to begin my day with over the last ten years; Dr. Michael Schwartz, psychiatrist, and the Reverend

Clayton Cobb, the Presbyterian minister, share amazing conversations with me as we run. These are really smart guys, and the friendship and intimacy of our communication represents one of the special bonding experiences of my life. Without my need for sports partners that blindness makes essential, I wouldn't necessarily know these men.

Certainly there are times when I wonder if I'm a burden to them—I mean, having to come pick me up in the mornings and guide me along the road—but this is the special part of the process because there's reciprocity in my turning disadvantage into advantage. If you ask them, I believe they'd say that they've grown from the experience, just as I have.

> There's reciprocity in my turning disadvantage into advantage.

I know my children have benefited greatly from having a blind father, though I also understand that there have been times it hasn't been easy. It's true, they are far more plugged into their senses than most people, but I think the contribution of my blindness to their lives, the advantage, as it were, of having had a blind parent, is also in their instinct and their willingness to always look for the best in others.

They both truly engage when meeting someone new. And as friends, they are remarkably loyal and committed to the people they love. Both of them are verbal. Boy, can they talk. From the time they were little, our dinner conversations were fantastic and opinionated. These are not softy Sullivans. They are strong, independent human beings, but they have a wonderful appreciation for everyone else whose lives they touch.

Now, let me be a little crass. Within my business life, blindness has turned out to be an amazing advantage. When I enter a meeting with a new client they're either uncomfortable with me or amazed at what they perceive to be my remarkable life. So, in the first half hour of the meeting I sort of own the stage. I've learned to try to negotiate points on a contract early on while folks are still off balance. Now, I admit this is taking advantage of you sighted people, and I'm kind of sorry, but honestly just a little sorry.

What's it really like to be married to a guy who's blind? I realized that I'd never really asked my wife that question, probably because I was afraid to know the answer. I finally built up the courage to talk about it. One night, at one of our favorite places to sit and talk, I asked, "Do you think there actually are advantages to spending your life with someone who's blind?"

Patty laughed quietly. "Well, I'll tell you this. When we first got married I used to try to give you the look. The look is when a woman is trying to tell her husband that he's way out of line; that he's wrong; that she disagrees or is disappointed.

"Obviously you didn't react, so I had to learn to talk to you, to verbalize all of my feelings, and it changed a young woman who was shy into a confident person who can express herself."

"That's pretty good," I said, relieved. "What else is unique or special about us?"

"Well," she went on, "I think the most important thing about us is our intimacy. I don't know that there are many couples who spend as much time talking as we do, and I love particularly our mornings together over coffee and the newspaper or a magazine article that we share."

Later in our conversation, she remarked, "I'm glad you can't see my face." She sighed. "It's getting old and haggard."

"Come on, Patty," I said. "You're as beautiful today—in fact, you're more beautiful today than you ever were. But I do wonder sometimes if it bothers you that I can't look at you."

"No," she said. "I know you see me. It's just that you see me in a different way."

"Inside out," I told her. "From the inside out."

And that was when this book was really born, when I realized that through my relationship with Patty I have come to appreciate the idea of life inside out, rather than outside in. The advantages of my blindness are multiple in nature, but essentially the most important advantage is in my openness to the world; in my lack of prejudice; in our intimacy.

> The most important advantage is in my openness to the world.

Patty is the catalyst that made me appreciate this most important premise in my life, but my relationship with my sister Peg really brings the point into even clearer focus. Because of the stress of our childhood and the fact that Peggy was eight years older and spent a lot of her teenage years responsible for her blind brother, I can't say that we were really close. Certainly, we loved each other, but we had never achieved real intimacy. I don't think I knew and understood my sister Peg until we were involved in two seminal events.

The first one was the death of our mother. Mom died twelve years ago after a long battle with cancer. Toward the end, I commuted from California to Boston to be with her as often as I could. Our older sister, Jean, lives in Florida, and though she tried hard, it wasn't always possible for her to be there. So, with Jean and me coming from different parts of the country, who had to step up? It was Peggy; in every way, she took care of our mother, and she did it selflessly. Despite being responsible for her own family she was always there. No request from my mother went unattended.

Now, Mom could be difficult. She had strong opinions, and she wasn't subtle, and as her cancer became more complex, she certainly wasn't always loving. But Peg just hung in there, not only willing to love our mother but willing to take a stand when necessary to get her the kind of care she needed.

Peg was, to put it simply, a rock. When I gave the eulogy for our mother, I talked a lot about my sister's strengths; and I remember sitting on her porch after the funeral when all the people were gone, talking with her about our lives and about how she believed taking care of me had made her a better person.

Now cut to eight years later. It was a few days before Thanksgiving when my phone rang and I heard my sister's voice. When you're blind, you can tell immediately where people are coming from just by their sound, their tone; and what I heard from Peggy that evening was fear.

"I have renal cancer," she said without any preamble. "They want to remove my kidney right away."

I couldn't believe it. *My rock has cancer, and it's serious.*

"What are they telling you?" I asked in a little voice.

"That it's advanced," she said. "They're suggesting I get my affairs in order."

I couldn't believe it. I remember shaking my head, trying to remove the cobwebs of my own fear, and then remembered all the times Peggy had been there to take care of me.

"Okay," I said, sounding stronger than I actually was. "We'll handle this together, sis."

From that moment on I became obsessed. I used every contact I had to chase down all the answers oncology could offer. I talked to doctors everywhere, learned as much as I could about the drugs that were available and the ones that were still in the pipeline, and in the process Peggy and I shared everything, including how she was feeling. And I don't mean physically; I mean how she was feeling psychologically. We talked about how she would express her love for her children and what she felt her husband needed from her in order to get through this crisis. In all of it we developed a bond stronger than steel and so resilient that even the threat cancer imposed could not sidetrack our shared love and commitment.

Peggy's still here, by the way, four years after her original diagnosis. She's not only surprising her doctors, but she's defying the odds, and her quality of life is terrific. She has oodles of grandchildren, and they all love her. Last Christmas Patty and I went back to Plymouth, Massachusetts, where Peggy lives, and shared one of the great family experiences of our lives. Peggy ran the show, and it was a holiday time of joy I'll never forget.

Even under the weight of life and death, human beings can find advantage in the possibilities, but you have to be willing to be open to the option. It's necessary to search for the advantages because on the surface life may look bleak. If you're only seeing the circumstance outside in, the future can look dim, but if your process works from inside out and involves your mind, heart, soul, instinct, and attitude—any disadvantage can be turned into an advantage.

> Even under the weight of life and death, human beings can find advantage in the possibilities.

I said at the beginning of this chapter that was my belief, and after writing all this down I'm even more convinced of it. Turning every disadvantage into an advantage is a choice each of us has to make, and essentially it is a simple choice, if you really think about it. What's the alternative? To wallow in sadness? To live in the negative? To disconnect from the unlimited possibilities of the human spirit? To reject engagement with others? To miss out on the possibilities of real love and sharing? Nobody wants to live like that.

What I'm convinced we want is to operate in the light, mirroring the best we see in others in ourselves. This process of give and take arises when we are able to turn every disadvantage into an advantage, because in our efforts we are engaging in a process that benefits all of us. My marriage to Patty would not be the great love it is if both of us had not grown into the idea of turning disadvantage to advantage. My children would have missed out on a lot had we not operated together to support the idea. And what about my sister Peg? Had Peggy not had to battle cancer, she and I would never have become as close as we are.

So, go out there and try it. Invest in it. Figure out how every circumstance in your life can be turned from disadvantage to advantage. I guarantee you'll be happier and much more fulfilled.

CHAPTER 12

Handi-Capable

MY MOTHER, God rest her soul, gambled. Thankfully, she never had enough money to hurt herself with her habit. My dad kept a pretty tight rein on the household expenses, and after he died I became her trustee and did the best I could to keep her habit in check. She was always buying scratch-off tickets, entering number pools, playing bingo, and waiting for me to get jobs performing in Las Vegas so she could show up and spend all of her dough—and some of my paycheck—on the slot machines. But with her gambling jones, the thing she loved the most was to go to the track and watch the ponies run.

She studied the racing form, knew the names of most of the jockeys, and had a pretty good grasp on who the good trainers were. When I went to Boston to visit her, we often ended up at Suffolk Downs racetrack or the Marshfield Fair, which had annual racing meets every summer. Even though the horses were older and not as good, Mom loved it.

It was through my mother that I came to understand the system of handicapping used in thoroughbred racing, and I found it amazing. The idea was that the better a horse became—by that I mean the number of wins or great performances—the more the animal was penalized by handicapping.

Jockeys in most states can't weigh over 115 pounds. The handicap system means that the jockey is weighed in, and then the better the horse, the more weight is added to his saddle, the theory being that this will make every race a closer competition.

So, for example, the baseline for some races is that the horse will be carrying 121 pounds but others in the race might be carrying up to 133 pounds—a 12-pound allowance being given to a "better horse" in order to slow him down.

When I learned about all this, after I told my mother I thought it was quite unfair, I thought about it and started to smile because this is the view I've taken of handicaps all my life. The handicapped person just needs to find a way to be better, smarter, and more committed and to have the kind of work ethic that allows all of us—54 million disabled citizens—in this country to take our rightful place here and in the rest of the world.

From Helen Keller to Stephen Hawking, from Christopher Reeve to my friend Stevie Wonder, there are people who have learned to take their handicaps—their disabilities—and through the application of an appropriate work ethic turn those disabilities into remarkable abilities.

Let me add that every person I've ever known, in one way or another, has a disability. Some are more obvious than others, but the truth is that all of us have a subtle, or not so subtle—and again, I'll use the word—handicap to overcome.

How did people like Helen Keller and Stevie Wonder do it? How did they decide to rise up, go against the grain, beat the odds? Was there some kind of formula, some system that's common to all of them; or was it just guts—sheer, unadulterated courage?

We all, whatever our disability, have to make the same decision; and that decision arises out of our belief in ourselves and the courage necessary to take a risk, a flyer, a chance, knowing that we can fail but understanding and believing that through failure we grow, we learn, we actuate all of our potential. We become more than we ever thought possible.

My insight in this chapter is that it is only through challenge that opportunity will present itself. Challenge is the engine that drives our success, and in the context of our challenges, even our fear works as a substantial motivator. My fear of failure has been as significant to my successes as my acceptance of new challenges, and in fact, somehow the two concepts seem to find a balance.

> My fear of failure has been as significant to my successes as my acceptance of new challenges.

A few years ago, Patty and I believed that our lives were on a positive track. I had a number of contracts that were paying us substantially; our children were out in the world; and Patty was very active giving her time to important nonprofit causes. So I certainly wasn't ready when our lives spun out of control in the course of one "black Friday."

At the time I had three principal relationships. I was under contact to a golf company, a major lecture agency, and Lions Club

International. First, the golf company declared bankruptcy—that ended that deal. Then the Lions Club got a new international president who wanted to go in a different direction. And the man who had created the speaker business that had made us a magnificent living decided to sell the company.

All of this happened on the same day. I remember being upstairs in our home, trying to console my inconsolable wife and at the same time trying to maintain my own sense of self-control. On that one afternoon my ability to make a living was taken away. In today's economy a lot of people are feeling the same thing. Their livelihoods have been pulled out from under them, even though it has nothing to do with their performance.

At a moment like this, human beings are truly challenged to the very depth of their souls. How do you dig out from under disasters? How do you cope when coping seems impossible? It's when you're able to say, *These challenges will lead to opportunities, I'm sure of it, if I bring a positive attitude to every conversation or experience.*

Here's an important truth: winning is as much an attitude as it is a performance. On that Friday I made a decision. I could not let my wife and family down. I needed to be inventive. I knew I needed to start by taking small but definite steps toward renewing our success.

> Winning is as much an attitude as it is a performance.

Within twenty-four hours I had hired a video editor and was building an online presence to market myself as a speaker. I immediately searched out a new agent and sold him on the idea that the best of Tom Sullivan was yet to come. There were three books I had wanted to write but had been too busy to begin. The next morning I sat down and outlined them all and within a week had sold the ideas to a major publisher.

Patty and I got busy going through our Rolodex of all of our friends, reminding them that my gifted spouse was a pretty terrific Realtor and that if they needed help finding or selling a home, she was the girl who could make it happen.

I called musician friends and let them know that I was back in business and available to perform with them or even to do backup work on any of their records.

Patty had always suggested that I should be doing voice-overs for commercials, so we went out and found an agent specializing in that very profitable kind of work.

Let me note that none of this energy was thrown out there randomly; we spent hours in those first few days mapping out a strategic plan. But the vital insight is that in a moment of crisis we chose to believe that the "handicap" of our circumstance was not stronger than the ability we could bring to bear to solve a problem.

Adversity truly does provide us with the greatest opportunity to win in the game of life, and playing the game is more fun than you can imagine. Even in the worst set of circumstances, I felt alive, motivated by the circumstance and convinced that I could overcome adversity by believing in the limitless possibilities that all of us possess.

The late Steve Jobs was fired from Apple but came back to create a technological revolution. The basketball player Michael Jordan was cut from his high school team but went on to become the greatest force in his sport. And here's the ultimate example: Walt Disney was fired by a local newspaper whose editor wrote that his dismissal was due to a lack of imagination. Wow.

If you think, though, that I have always risen above adversity—frankly, that is not the case.

When Patty and I moved to Colorado to be with our adult children, I basically left show business behind, and in the process I got out of the habit of having to compete for the jobs I wanted. After a six-year stay in Denver, we moved back to Southern California, and I began trying to sell my wares in the industry that had once welcomed me.

The funny part about show business is that it really is an occupation where if you are out of sight, you are out of mind. As you grow older, the executives you call on seem to get younger, and in fact, many of the network programmers I visited couldn't even remember television before 1980. It's a shame that so many writers get put out to pasture when they still have so much to offer; but that's the way it is, and in the late eighties, in the eyes of the executives, I had lost the eye of the tiger.

When I was young, calling on the same kind of executives, I would walk in assuming that I would always get the job, that they would have to hire me, that their network just couldn't get along without me. This time I came in with maturity, which basically meant that I assumed I had no value anymore.

If you accept your handicap as a limitation, you'll get just what you deserve, and that's what happened to me—until I became competitively angry when I dealt with the bully in my backyard. Ah, now that's a healthy thing.

As I've mentioned, there are two kinds of anger: one is destructive, leading you nowhere; and one is competitive, taking you anywhere you want to go. Thank goodness the eye of the tiger came back, and that's why Patty and I were able to overcome "black Friday" and move forward with our lives.

So, we need to accept our limitations but acknowledge that

we have the right to expectations. I believe that over time, I've achieved a balance between a realistic view of my disability and a wonderful celebration of my ability. If we acknowledge the premise that everyone does have a handicap, we can be far more sensitive to each other's imperfections and much more in tune with the specialness of the other, which makes relationships, love, and friendship possible for all of us. Looking at the complexity of our circumstance from inside out provides us with the vision to make good choices and frame our future around the possible, rather than the impossible.

> We need to accept our limitations but acknowledge that we have the right to expectations.

CHAPTER 13

The Man in the Mirror

AS I'VE GROWN OLDER I've realized, boy, there sure is a lot that I don't know much about. I mean, I'm writing this book and giving you a blind man's look at life inside out, but in the process I've realized how much I really don't understand about the world of vision. I certainly know nothing about colors, and the idea of a rainbow is, frankly, just unfathomable. When I try and consider what it must be like to see, I can't even imagine it.

The other day I was down on the beach with my son as he was getting ready to go surf. Just before he paddled out to hang ten or whatever they do out there, he commented that he saw a large freighter moving along the coastline. I asked him how far away it was.

"Oh, gee, Dad," he said, "it has to be four or five miles out there."

Four or five miles? I couldn't believe it.

I said, "Well, it must be a very clear day today, right?"

He said, "Oh, yeah. I can see all around the peninsula, all the way to the tip of Catalina Island."

"Wait a minute," I said, amazed, "that's twenty-six miles away. You can't really see it, can you?"

"I can see the shape, Dad. I can't make out things that are on the island, but I know it's out there and I can get a picture of it."

It doesn't happen very often, but there are times when I really would like to have the gift of sight, and yet these pages are full of concepts that have made my view of life inside out a wonderful experience. When I got home that morning from the beach, Patty was getting dressed and putting on her makeup.

"Is it hard to do that?" I asked.

"What do you mean?" she said, laughing.

"I mean, is it difficult to put on makeup?"

"Not if you've got the right light," she told me, "and a good mirror."

At that moment it dawned on me that I had no idea what a mirror was. So, I Googled it. Have you ever gone online to look something up and learned much more than you ever wanted to know? Reading about the history of mirrors, I was surprised to find out that many different materials have been used to reflect people's images back to themselves, starting with some guy in the caveman era looking in a stream and seeing his reflection. Over thousands of years, polished stone, various kinds of metal, and obviously glass have gone into the creation of mirrors, and man has been looking at himself through these objects for many millenniums.

I thought about the Snow White fairy tale and the queen asking the mirror who was the fairest one of all. The thing is, when the queen looked in the mirror and had to face her reflection, she wasn't too happy. Did she learn anything else about herself, or was it only a visual impression?

I decided it was time for me to create my own mirror, not made of metal or glass; actually, not made out of any material at all. My mirror was going to be defined by scrupulous self-assessment, and like the mirror at my wife's makeup table, the picture that would look back at me had to be accurate.

As I began to look into a blind man's mirror, the first question I asked was how I felt about the image looking back at me. On the whole, I guess I felt pretty good about myself, based on a critical decision I had made a few years earlier. Somewhere along the way I had decided that the true test of my self-worth was measured by the way I treated others.

Here's how I had come to see life's process when assessing whether or not to take a particular course of action. I began to frame my choices around this question: *selfish* or *selfless?* Was what I wanted based only on my own selfish desire, or was I selfless in the way I made choices? By *selfless,* I mean did I make a decision based on

> I began to frame my choices around this question: *selfish* or *selfless?*

how it affected me, or was I willing to take into consideration how my desire would affect anyone else who might be involved? I figured out that on the whole I was working to live my life selflessly, rather than selfishly, and I have found that this conduct of character provides all of us with a very strong and consistent self-image.

Years ago when I was working for *Good Morning America,* ABC wanted me to move to New York to be closer to the show and to my assignments. I was certainly intrigued by the opportunity. It would mean a new contract and more money and the chance to guest-host when Charlie Gibson was on vacation or away on assignment. I remember coming home and telling Patty and the children about the opportunity.

Right away Tom was brokenhearted. He is really a California kid, a water baby who loves and appreciates everything about the ocean. Blythe was about to enter high school and was very involved in the love of her horses and sports of all kinds. Patty had created an organization of very gifted women called Vistas for Blind Children and was active raising money for a little school called the Blind Children's Center in Los Angeles.

So, the reaction of my family was not what I would call a ringing endorsement. I immediately made the selfless decision, and it wasn't hard. Obviously, I love my family more than life, so here we are, still in California.

Ironically, the next year ABC was sold, and all of us who had become members of what we used to think of as the *Good Morning America* family had our contracts terminated in a cost-saving move. So, had we gone to New York we would have given up far more than we got back. It's odd, but usually the selfless choice not only turns out to be the right one from the standpoint of our character, but also from the standpoint of the end result.

My next reveal from looking in a blind man's mirror occurred when I considered how I was treated by others. We use phrases like, "what you give is what you get back" or "what goes around comes around," and these phrases are truly ap-

> The attitude you project to the world is generally bounced right back to you.

plicable when you look in the mind's eye mirror. Like *selfish* and *selfless*, the attitude you project to the world, both individually and to a group, is generally bounced right back to you.

I choose to live my life willing to risk by extending to others, and in general I try not to create expectations about what I'm going to get back. However, in at least nine out of ten considered cases, I've received far more than I've given.

I've often been fortunate helping a number of young people acquire their first career break. I suppose it's because I've worked for so many corporations as a speaker and kept an effective network of human resource people and corporate CEOs that I'm able to be helpful to these talented young people.

I can't tell you how many times one of these gifted young men or women has grown in his or her business life and then turned around and hired old Tom Sullivan for commercials or speeches or consulting work. One of the truths that you see in the mirror is that you really do get more than you give.

Looking deeper at my reflection, the picture looking back at me isn't always the person I'd like him to be. I have to admit that I sometimes judge people too quickly and launch into relationships expecting too much. I also am far too opinionated and can become too critical when I've been disappointed. Though blindness has made me a good listener, I'm still nowhere near as patient as I need to be, and the mirror in my mind clearly reflects that I am much, much too impulsive. And for a blind person, that can be dangerous. I remember as if it were yesterday being at a meeting in New York City with a book publisher that hadn't gone well. Coming out of the skyscraper with my guide dog, Edison, we came to the corner at the height of five o'clock traffic. I was impatient and irritated by the events of my day, and so rather than waiting for the light to change, since I didn't hear cars coming around the corner I told the dog "forward" and stepped into the street. Thank God the animal was not suffering with my impatience. He froze, performing what's called a traffic check. He would not let me go forward, and the whizzing taxicab that passed within inches of my feet blew his horn in protest, but I was safe. Impatience is my worst character trait, and I constantly have to work to hold it in check. This problem is exacerbated by a large smudge on the glass of my mirror. It's called ego, and though all successful people have to have one, mine sometimes gets out of whack, and Patty has to straighten me out, which she does without hesitation.

The other thing I have come to understand as I look in the mirror is that, though for the most part I operate selflessly, I tend to be too quick to throw away opinions that don't immediately gel with mine. A few years ago my wife and I were completely engaged reading the late president Ronald Reagan's diaries. One of the constant themes of this great communicator surprised me. Though there was no doubt about where he stood on issues or principles, he was remarkably open and patient, listening to the folks on the other side of the aisle or talking with other world leaders.

For example, though he called the Soviet Union an evil empire and demanded that President Gorbachev tear down the Berlin Wall, they still found a way to sign a nuclear test ban treaty, and after both had left office they actually became good friends. Why? I believe that this great president understood the power that could be gained by listening to the other fellow's point of view and having the patience to maintain his position while searching for compromise.

The other thing I found important as I considered the image in my mental mirror was whether or not I took myself too seriously. It's so important to be able to laugh, not only at someone else's joke but at the circumstance you find yourself in. People without an appropriate sense of humor cannot get out of their own way, cut themselves a little slack, and really find the path to enjoying life. We often tend to be so embarrassed in certain circumstances that we forget to see the real funniness of the moment.

> People without an appropriate sense of humor cannot find the path to enjoying life.

If you're lucky enough to work on a television series, you would be amazed at how performers use humor to break the tension of the work. One of my favorite moments early in my career was when I did an episode of *Mork & Mindy* with the incredible Robin Williams. For those who don't remember, the series was about an alien who comes to earth and learns of our culture in his own odd way. In my episode, Robin's character, Mork, is supposed to learn what it's like to be blind. Robin was struggling with being funny because he kept seeing the serious nature of disability and didn't want to make fun of it. I finally told him that I loved to laugh at my disability, so in our next scene he borrowed my guide dog's harness, took his shirt off, and crawled out on the stage, pretending to be my guide dog. The audience and Tom Sullivan convulsed with laughter as I patted his back and kept saying "Good dog, Robin, good dog."

I have a lot of friends who love silent films, particularly the comedies with Charlie Chaplin, Buster Keaton, and Harold Lloyd. What they seem to find most fun about these early movies is watching a great comic get into a situation with innocence and complicate it by struggling to work his way out. To my friends, that struggle to overcome embarrassment is real comedy, and life needs to be lived with a smile, a wink, and a nod.

It's important that the picture looking back at you in any mirror reflects the simplest but most profound of all human values. Do you love others as much as you love yourself? The real test of character as seen through a blind man's mirror is whether in all of these values we extend to the other as much love as we maintain for ourselves. All the concepts suggested in this examination come together in the inside-out view that it's critically important to love the other with the same passion you feel about yourself.

This premise fits the tenets of many of the world's great religions and ancient philosophies. Learning to love openly is not easy because it requires risk in order to gain reward. We risk rejection. We risk being misunderstood. We must risk disappointment and heartache, but none of these is difficult if the basic picture returning in the mind's-eye mirror is of a person whose love for others equals love of self.

The principle is certainly profound and yet simple in the beauty of its conception, but the application is never easy, and we often fail based on the foibles of jealously and envy. Yet through the

> We can work toward the perfection of a beautiful soul.

scrutiny available in the mind's eye mirror we can continue to work toward the perfection of a beautiful soul, though perfection is impossible.

I know my wife is beautiful, but every day as she stands before her makeup mirror she complains about a line on her face or crow's-feet under her eyes or her skin not being tight enough.

136

I think she's crazy. For me she's the most beautiful woman in the world; and yet, as she studies herself in the mirror and considers her reflection she makes ongoing decisions that she hopes can enhance her appearance.

I use the mind's mirror in the same way, holding my character up for continuous scrutiny and constantly working to be a better man, husband, father, and friend. The wonderful thing about looking in the mirror is that it not only provides us with the ability to observe ourselves but invites us to grow, and return again and again to take another look and feel better about who we are. It empowers us to live richly from the inside out.

CHAPTER 14

Here's Looking at You

HERE'S LOOKING AT YOU, KID.

Humphrey Bogart looks over the rim of his glass in a smoke-filled bar at the beautiful Ingrid Bergman and states that famous phrase. His eyes take in her face, and as before he is struck by the luminescent beauty he sees there. There's a direct connection between what he sees and what he feels in his heart. The immediacy of the visual picture creates an inner stirring of romance; of love won and love lost; of Casablanca.

All my life I've been fascinated by the relationship between what you see and what you perceive, and frankly a lot of it is hard for me to understand. The concept of people falling in love at first glance across a crowded room is impossible for me to grasp. What is it that the eyes convey, and how do they do it? In fact, facial expressions in general are impossible for me to get a handle on. I mean, what is a wink? What does it mean when someone says she's batting her eyes at you or, as I noted earlier in this text, one spouse is giving the other "the look"?

My world of recognition as a blind person is as different to you as your world of visuals is to me. I understand that based on the questions kids ask me. Little children want to know if blind people really dream, and they all are convinced that I must see the color black because when they close their eyes, that's what they see.

Almost all young people are sad when they think about my being blind because, like their adult counterparts, they believe I've been cheated, that being blind is a burden, and that I'm not being given the opportunity to enjoy the world the same way they do. They're right; but you know, I kind of like the inside-out way I see the world.

Let's start with my sense of three dimensions. I've never been able to grasp how an artist paints depth. I mean, to me it's all just lines on a canvas. My sense of dimension comes from being able to hold something in my hand. I remember as a child learning shapes with blocks, and those shapes turned into understanding the use of space when I moved around my house and converted the rectangular block to the rectangular shape of a room. To be able to grasp the size of a skyscraper or a football stadium, I've actually had to walk around them or go up an elevator, open a window and hear how far it is to the ground.

As a child I spent a lot of time touching things. I've heard it said that the eyes are the window on the soul. Well, my hands provided me with the awareness of almost everything I needed to know. There are major gaps in my knowledge base. For example, I love animals, yet there are so many species that I'll never have the chance to touch and so cannot really learn much about them. My sense of distance is based on how long it takes me to get somewhere, and that means that I have to know how fast we're moving. My father and mother said I did constant projections on how long a trip would take in my dad's big old Oldsmobile. Well, that was because that was the only way I felt connected to the reality of our travel and the speed that we needed to apply to get there.

I suppose the best example of this adjustment in my awareness is when I'm on an airplane. Here I am, thirty thousand feet in the air, zooming over the ground at over five hundred miles an hour, and yet there's really no sense of movement. My guide dog doesn't even know what it means to be up in the air, since he doesn't ever look out the window. I think he thinks he's just in some kind of big moving car, and it certainly doesn't seem to cause any undue alarm.

There's stuff that just makes me go *wow*. I was working as a performer in Lake Tahoe, and I met Bertha the elephant, who was the opening act on the show. I mean, I really met her up close and personal, and I think we became friends. For some reason she loved to eat cigars, so I always had one in my pocket when I visited her. The trainer let me interact with this amazing animal, and I couldn't believe how big she was or how amazing her skin felt under my hands. And then there was the length of her tongue or how well she could use her trunk to pick up tiny things. No question about it, Bertha was really a big wow.

We could go on and on with these examples of the things I don't know, but I think in this chapter it would be more instructive for me to try to articulate how I look at you. Let's see if I can illuminate the picture for you.

Patty always tells me that no two people look the same, even if it's a celebrity impersonator. Well, that's exactly the way it is with voices. No two people sound alike, and I've been able to file away thousands of voice imprints in the same way you file faces in your consciousness. There are some generalized patterns that are worth examining.

Most men and women with dark hair have huskier and slightly lower-pitched speaking tones than those who are light-skinned or blond. I think this is largely because of the areas in Europe they come from, and though it's a general concept, it does tend to hold true.

Also, no two speech patterns are exactly alike. By that I mean the rhythm of speech and the intonation and accent that goes along with it. Using the voice as a reference I also tune into the height of the person. That's not hard to do in relationship to my own height.

Then there's this wonderful little trick some blind people use—and I'm one of them—called facial vision. It's the same premise that a bat applies when it moves through space in the dark. As you walk, you create vibration by moving air, and that vibration bounces from the object or person to the facial area, adding to the picture you're gaining. This system of facial vision—or blind person's sonar—is very useful when traveling to find doorways into buildings, trees, signposts, and basically anything that can be reflected by sound.

Body carriage says a great deal. Physically fit people tend to carry their chins higher with their shoulders back. It's part of the posture of good health.

I said before that a smile really does have a sound, and it will always be my favorite, particularly when it comes from a child. So often people think that I miss the subtext of what they're really feeling because I have no visual sense to draw on. They couldn't be more wrong. When I'm in a meeting I can hear someone tapping on the desk because they're in a hurry. I can tell when a person sits back in their chair bored or breaks off eye

> A smile really does
> have a sound, and
> it will always be
> one of my favorites.

contact because they disagree with what I'm saying. The counterpart to that is that I also get it when people are enthused because I can hear them lean forward and can tell by the sound of their voice that they're focusing completely on what I'm trying to get across.

And the human voice—ah, the human voice—it never lies; or, rather, because of the nuance in the voice I never miss a lie or any form of fabrication when it's being offered in an interaction or negotiation. The bottom line is: nobody is *that* fine an actor. Something in a person's sound will always give away the truth, the absolute of a conversation. Sincerity is obvious, but so is a lie.

I'm constantly surprised at the things people tell me. It's sort of like being a Catholic priest and hearing people's confessions. I think because I can't see them they feel safe. It's as if they believe there's a screen up between me and them, and, as in the confessional, they can unburden their sins to Father Tom. This particularly happens on airplanes. On cross-country flights from L.A. to New York I have heard some amazing stories that will not be included in these pages.

I spend a lot of time listening to the way people walk because hearing people's footfalls can reveal how much confidence they feel in themselves. It's not just a question of how fast or slow they move but more the body lean and purpose defined by the step. Now, there is a variable here, based on age, sex, and size, but in confident walkers there's always a forward lean, an attitude, and it's not difficult to pick up on.

Take the time to listen to the sound of people's breathing,

and you'll understand a lot about their overall health and attitude. Certainly, there are exceptions; people with asthma or lung disease obviously sound different, but for the most part you can read people's health, their physical well-being, by just studying their breathing patterns. Understanding a person's state of mind is based largely on what they say, but their rapidity, pitch, and vocal projection can also tell you a lot about the security or insecurity that a person is really feeling.

All of these things go into a blind person's portrait, and though it's not a painting on a canvas, my mind's-eye picture, I believe, is pretty accurate.

So, about this idea that the eyes are the window on the soul, whether that's just a poetic metaphor or a truism, I'm not sure. What I do know is that understanding a person's real character can happen in all kinds of marvelous ways, and a blind person's snapshots range all the way from the significance of handshakes and hugs to something as odd as a person's smell.

> A blind person's snapshots range from handshakes and hugs to a person's smell.

Nervousness is registered through sweat, and I can pick up on that stuff as well as any hunting dog. Also, have you ever noticed that certain colognes or perfumes fit people's skin types? When they get it right they tend to exude more confidence. I wear Aramis aftershave, and it fits me perfectly. Patty is a Chanel girl. When she's tried other perfumes they just didn't fit her skin tone, and something as trivial as this can make a difference in—and I know this concept is a little out there—your aura, the overall feeling you give off to every other person who comes in contact with you. I remember when I met Patty, there was an immediate mutual attraction, a release of pheromones. We just knew that we were falling in love.

To a blind person with educated insight and effective instinct, most human beings are pretty transparent, and my picture of who you are is as complete as I need it to be. I don't want to seem naïve about this. Of course I'd love to see Patty and my children, and I would enjoy checking out the faces of a lot of you who will be reading this book. I'm not trying to suggest that it wouldn't be wonderful to see people exactly the same way you do, but I actually think that I'm plugging in even more information, utilizing all of my senses, along with this inner vision that has become so much a part of my life.

I've had so many friends try to describe visuals to me, and I understand that their hearts are in the right place as they battle to put words around the concept of color, a sunset, a Christmas tree all lit up in a house full of love. In fact, the basic concept of light and dark is impossible for anyone to articulate to any blind person.

Some of the concepts I'm talking about in these pages may seem difficult to grasp. The difference is that you hold the option to work on it, to take in this information and use it, and in doing so enrich your lives in ways that up until now you may not have even considered.

Remember, earlier I suggested that you plug in your senses. Here I'm encouraging the possibility of opening up the world of beauty and awareness in ways that are virtually limitless and go beyond simple sensory awareness. It's going to take work. I want to be clear about that. Plugging in the insight information that will allow you to expand the scope of your awareness doesn't happen just because you decide. It takes practice.

Recently, I spent three days with a Fortune 500 corporate group of managers teaching them how to listen effectively in a phone conversation. Within a short time, they began to read the nuances expressed by people who were either happy, sad, frustrated, disappointed, or angry. They quickly understood that they could gain great advantages in a conversation by turning up their appreciation for the subtleties of speech that really were quite obvious. All of our senses can be applied with far more attention to detail in framing our human understanding.

In Winter Park, Colorado, the National Sports Center for the Disabled has taught over a hundred and fifty thousand disabled people to ski, representing over 140 different disabilities, blindness being one of them. The Sullivans have spent thirty Christmases in this wonderful mountain environment, and we treasure our time together as Blythe or Sully guides me down slopes. My children have been doing that since they were very little. Tom was only seven and Blythe was nine when they first began copying the instructors and learning to guide their dad.

In contrast, many of the volunteers who give their time tirelessly to the Winter Park program learn to guide blind people as adults, and it is fascinating to watch the first time they ski under blindfolds. I have actually witnessed volunteers freeze when they're asked to go down a hill with their eyes covered, tethered and safe based only on the sound of their guide's voice. It scares them to death. I've seen the same thing happen to friends of mine when the lights are turned out and a room goes dark.

Look, it's not easy to be blind, and just putting on a blindfold or spending time in the dark doesn't teach the stuff I'm talking about. Seeing life inside out will happen by focusing on one thing at a time. As I suggested earlier, take a day and concentrate on one of the other four senses. See how much you can learn.

Pay closer attention to the sound of voices on a phone call and work to assess their moods. Check out handshakes or hugs to get a physical manifestation of where people are coming from when you're dealing with them, and work to discover a uniqueness in every human being, rather than falling into the trap of labeling them.

This new world of inside-out vision is a wonderful place to live in, so go ahead, take a chance, give it a try. There's nothing to lose and so much to gain.

> Work to discover a uniqueness in every human being.

Oh, by the way, here's a little note of honesty, though I hate to admit it. I envy you. I'm extremely jealous of your ability to enjoy the beauty of that sunset or a rainbow or the change of seasons or the face of someone you love. But I've come to terms with all of those things and come to treasure life as I see it; and now I'm delighted to encourage you to take a different look inside out.

CHAPTER 15

Faith

I WAS IN NORTH CAROLINA playing in the Duke Children's Classic, a golf tournament that invited celebrities along with professionals to raise money for eye research for this prestigious institution.

I was on the driving range, extremely nervous because I was surrounded by some of the great names in golf, and right next to me—oh my, right next to me—was Slammin' Sammy Snead—Samuel Jackson Snead, arguably one of the five greatest players in the history of this sport. Mr. Sam, as he was called, was known for many things. It was said that he was the cheapest man alive and that he still had the first dollar that he'd ever made. It was also said that he never did anything for free, especially give golf lessons to amateurs.

So, there I was, supposed to hit my puny little golf shots right next to the great master. I stood in awe listening to Sam swing the golf club and whistle to himself while he did it, and there was a consistency in the way he whistled through his teeth. It was always in perfect three-quarter waltz time, and that's how he swung the club—in beautiful, smooth, precise waltz time.

Mr. Sam was in his early seventies when I met him, but the swing was still silky smooth, and after he practiced for a while I finally had the courage to say good morning. Surprisingly, Sam Snead took a real interest in me and actually spent a half hour working on my technique. Nobody on the range could believe it. At the end of thirty minutes I offered to pay him for his time, not wanting to be insulting but remembering what people had told me about his approach to amateurs.

"Forget it, boy," he said. "This lesson's on me."

"Thank you," I said, not knowing what else to say.

Before walking away he turned and said quietly, "Consider this lesson on account."

"On account?" I queried.

"On account of the fact that my eyes aren't very good anymore, son. I'm just at the end of playing this game, but watching you today, well, it gave me the faith to believe that maybe I could keep going for a little while longer."

The faith to believe; the grace to cope with any circumstance life presents; the hope that the human spirit will overcome all things if you believe in God's love and in the grace He provides to all of us at all times and in every circumstance: these have become the cornerstone, the foundation, the rock of my inside-out vision. It is the most important insight I've discovered, but it sure didn't come easily.

For many years I denied loving God, and in that way I suppose I denied not only His love but His grace. Why? Because I felt sorry for myself. I was blind, wasn't I? I was dealt a bad hand from the bottom of the deck, a bad roll of the dice, a bad break. Circumstance, or maybe even God himself, had made me blind.

> What I understood very early was that I was going to have to work harder just to be equal.

I wasn't sure. What I understood very early was that the world viewed me as different and that I was going to have to work harder just to be equal. My life would be a constant making-up for my disability as I struggled against the odds that society had placed in my way.

Then, gradually, success became a pattern. I found out that I was pretty smart and could do very well academically. I learned that I was athletic and could excel at the sports I chose. There was also music. And Billy Hannon became my first friend, the boy who asked me to play with him. Talents began to emerge. People liked it when I sang, and I found out that I could become a pretty good songwriter if I gave it my best. All of this required hard work, none of it came easy, but there was a constant rewarding of my efforts.

Sometimes I think God works for us, even if we don't acknowledge it, and it's clear to me now, looking back, that my life has been grace-filled. God has been on my side all the time, even if I was too blind to see it, even if I lacked the insight to thank Him. (I wasn't always living from the inside out, unfortunately.)

Let me hasten to say there were extenuating circumstances. I grew up as a conservative Irish

> God has been on my side all the time, even if I was too blind to see it.

Catholic in Boston. It was fish on Friday and confession on Saturday afternoon. Billy Hannon and I would be forced by our parents to show up at the Holy Name Church and go through the process of sliding down the pews, getting closer and closer to the confessional, getting closer and closer to having to confess our sins, and all of it creating inside me a horrible sense of guilt.

About what? You know, I really don't understand any of that. What could an eleven-year-old boy be really guilty about? But if you're conditioned to believe that you're not worthy of God's love, well, that's the way you begin to think. Sin and salvation; boy, I got a lot of those. Then there were Mass and Communion on Sundays, along with morning and night prayers with my mother scrupulously supervising. Growing up, for me God was never a force of love but a force of judgment, and I guess I didn't know how I would ever earn His love.

It was when I attended Providence College two years before going on to Harvard that God manifested something like the beginnings of a reality in my life. I got to know the priests who worked to educate me, and for the most part these were spectacular people. I found myself beginning to think that maybe God could demonstrate His love for us if we were just open to the possibility.

And then there was Patty. My wife's faith is absolute and unshakable. Its essence is found in her gratitude for what she's been given by God. As I began to come to terms with my blindness and recognize that I did have a real place in the world, and that the world could be a wonderful place, I found myself believing that I wasn't achieving any of my goals alone. There had to be a force for good that was a constant as I was moving forward on my life's journey.

And then, as you read, I faced the ultimate life-changing moment when our daughter fell in the swimming pool. In that horrific experience, I came to understand the miracle of God's grace. No angel reached down and plucked Blythe out of the water. No, I asked for God's intervention—I begged for it—and I received it through my own capacity to hear the sound of her air bubbles, follow them, dive down, and bring her to the surface, respirating her and finally hearing the blessed sound when she breathed. In that moment, that microcosm of life and faith, I understood that God could work through me, through my willingness and engagement in whatever circumstance I was being presented with.

> In that moment, I understood that God could work through me.

Since that day in June over thirty years ago, I have never doubted the role of God's grace in my life. My faith isn't perfect, and certainly in these pages I'm not purporting to be a theologian or even a member of any organized church. But my simple belief that God loves me and offers me the grace to find the way to eternal life with Him in heaven is the simple premise that has become the foundation of my existence here on earth.

I have even come to determine that God has a plan for me. I believe I was placed here as a blind person to develop the insight, the courage, and the commitment to change the way people see the world and view disability. God has offered me a path to purpose and the grace to make the most of my journey. It now becomes my responsibility to understand His purpose for me and to demonstrate the courage to follow the path of faith that He has offered.

I also want to note that though my faith has become an absolute, a real commitment, I'm not trying to indicate in these pages—or anywhere else for that matter—that life should be a process of working to obtain perfection. That's reserved for God and for His love. I fail constantly, and more often than not the things I desire don't happen.

Show business, maybe more than any other industry, is a constant pattern of rejection and disappointment, and I'm not saying that if you believe in God's grace, every circumstance in life will turn out exactly the way you hope it will. I don't think that's realistic. But the affirmation through your faith that you'll always have enough grace to grow in love and faith is a constant, and it empowers a life lived inside out.

> You'll always have enough grace to grow in love and faith.

Let me frame it this way. If I spent every morning and every night saying a prayer that someday I would play center field for the Boston Red Sox, it's still just not going to happen. My prayer is unrealistic. The insight of my faith relates specifically to the belief that God does have a plan for me and for all of us, but it's up to me and up to you to open our eyes, ask for the grace, and believe in His commitment that He will always point the way if we just have the insight to understand, trust His love, and accept that His grace is bountiful and constant.

If you think I'm right, doesn't it make you feel good—I mean loved, secure? And doesn't it make you believe in the unlimited possibilities of the human spirit to just go for it, to reach for the goal, to love playing the game of life with all of its possibilities and to take every gift that God has presented us with, explore it, and use it to its fullest, knowing that that's exactly what He wants for us? He wants us to make the most of His grace, He wants us to become the best persons we can be, and I have come to believe that He wants us to join Him in eternal life in heaven.

If the soul is the essence of who we are in God's plan, then it's through a life spent inside out that we will find the ability to gain greater understanding of what He has in mind for each of us.

CHAPTER 16

Challenge: The Gateway to Opportunity

HERE'S A NEWS FLASH. The bullet point. My ultimate insight. You're not ever going to engage in life as a winner—live life from the inside out—if you're not driven by the essential element of challenge.

Earlier in this book I talked about turning disadvantages into advantages, and I believe that every disability in life can be turned into an ability, without exception. I have no doubt about that concept, but none of us will carry out that principal belief unless we're willing to accept the operational idea that we are personally motivated when presented with challenges; it is challenge that stimulates us to perform at our best.

> It is challenge that stimulates us to perform at our best.

We often hear athletes talk about performing on the big

stage. Years ago, Michael Jordan and Larry Bird always wanted the ball at the end of an NBA game so they could take the last shot. Tiger Woods has often spoken of how he gets into the zone over a putt on eighteen to win a major tournament. John Elway once told me that when he played in Super Bowl games for the Denver Broncos, the opportunity of challenge allowed him to slow the game down, be more in touch, to focus his concentration in a way that made him a much better player and allowed his team to win back-to-back Super Bowls in the late nineties.

What's the old phrase? *When the going gets tough, the tough get going.* What becomes central to this theme of challenge is to be able to break it down into categories, because each challenge requires a different kind of effort in order to turn it into an opportunity.

What did it take, for example, for young Tom Sullivan to find his way out of darkness and into the light of a life so full of joy and adventure? First—and I think foremost in the acceptance of challenge—is the idea that the desire to try has to overcome, to trump any fear you might have of failure. I like to think of this as the "want" factor. You just have to want it. And then you have to be willing to risk everything to try.

You've often heard people say failure is not an option, but human beings do fail, even when their attention is focused and their preparation is excellent. We all fail, but here's the secret. In failure we find the learning curve necessary to grow and succeed. And more than that, the joy of living, the juice that we get from being alive, the zing, the pizzazz, along with the major element of wow, comes when failure and disappointment have eventually led to success and achievement. Remember that Thomas Alva Edison engaged in over a thousand experiments

> In failure we find the learning curve necessary to grow and succeed.

before, *voilà*! Electricity moved and the light bulb worked. So, it all comes together when attitude connects with aptitude.

Finding out that I was musical allowed me to excel, and not just in the classical field; I was the young guy who could play at parties and dances during my teenage years. And, boy, was that handy when I was trying to get to know some pretty girl who was going out with the captain of the football team.

In sports I had to search for something I could do better than most other kids. And it was wrestling, something you didn't have to see to be good at. I also realized that I had a chance to excel in academics and that it was okay to be a little geeky and appreciate Shakespeare from an early age.

I suppose as you read these words you might be thinking, *Sure, it was okay for you, Sullivan. You had extra gifts, extra talents; God had been good to you.* I remember a story my father told me when I was a little boy. You all know it—the story with the tortoise and the hare. Slow and steady wins the race, right? And you know what? That really is the truth. The flash and dash of life won't ever bring the consistency necessary to stick to something you believe in and get to the finish line. Physical challenges require patience and the willingness to practice in order to overcome any adversity.

And then what about mental challenges? Aren't our brains wonderful? A human being's capacity to work out complex mental challenges is pretty remarkable when you think about it. I do my best thinking in the shower when I'm trying to come up with a theme for a speech that I have to give. For some reason, as the hot water rolls over my body, my brain seems to kick in, and thoughts flow freely.

Also, because I'm a songwriter, I constantly seem to come up with musical ideas when I'm asleep. They jolt me awake, and my wife has often found me sitting up in bed with a small cassette machine in my hand singing something in the middle of the night so that I won't forget it the next morning.

Mental challenges require cerebral focus. You've just got to get the old brain ticking. But also, I think there are moments when you have to allow it to—I'm quoting my son—chill out. There are times when you have to give a mental challenge a rest. It's amazing how much our brains are like computers. They lock up. They glitch. They shut down, and when that happens, hey, just give it a rest.

It's been said that Albert Einstein slept only two or three hours a night. What people sometimes forget to note is that history has shown that he took a two-hour nap every afternoon. Why? Because this genius needed to give his brain a rest. Overcoming mental challenges is about as satisfying as life gets. And though you may not get the endorphin release that comes from physical exercise, I've found that when I solve a complex problem, I just can't keep a smile off my face. I'll bet you're the same.

> When I solve a complex problem, I just can't keep a smile off my face.

Overcoming emotional challenges is not as cut-and-dried in terms of the formula that brings a satisfying solution. In an emotional challenge there's also a chemical quotient to deal with—as in, let's say, a person's struggle with bipolar syndrome. There's also an interactive component in the relationship you have with another person. Getting along with a coworker, problems in a marriage, interaction with your children—relational challenges will always have many detours and complications that keep them from being as simple as moving from point A to point B in the execution of turning challenge into opportunity.

Remember, you can't control where another person is coming from. You can only hope to direct the interaction toward a positive outcome.

And then there are our spiritual challenges. Everyone I know has had moments in which their faith has been truly tested. Maybe that's what God had in mind. Maybe, just maybe, this life is a test, a grand experiment that God, in His infinite wisdom, offers us. Maybe in a subtle way achieving oneness with Him in heaven, as it were—paradise, eternal life—is really our ultimate challenge.

I haven't found anything to support this idea in Scripture, but I have a feeling that in the essence of our creation we

> The opportunity for our success is boundless.

were meant to be challenged. I mean, didn't Adam and Eve have to earn the right to stay in the garden? They blew it, didn't they? And now here we are, challenged on every front, and yet the opportunity for our success is boundless.

As a baby boomer I share a lot of conversations with friends who are talking about their golden years, and what I have found amazing is the difference in attitude between those who look at retirement as a career change and those who say, "I just can't wait to retire." The other day a friend was telling me that in the two years since he left his corporation he was already sick of playing golf, and he wasn't too happy about another trip his wife was planning so that they could take a class in French cooking in Provence.

I'm not putting down the idea of a relaxing retirement. What I'm trying to express passionately is that all of us will dry up and blow away in the wind if we're not constantly challenging ourselves—our attitudes, our values, our way of doing things. We will always need challenge to feel well, to feel alive.

> We will always need challenge to feel alive.

Looking inside out at life takes on appropriate importance when you realize that somewhere in yourself is the drive necessary to become active, engaged, involved, and fulfilled.

A few years ago I had the opportunity to spend time with the comedy legend George Burns. Mr. Burns was in his mid-nineties, and I've never met anyone who was more disciplined or made better use of every minute of his time. For George Burns, time really mattered. He knew he was coming to the end of his life, but even with the clock ticking he was preparing for a performance when he turned a hundred at Caesar's Palace in Las Vegas.

Every day Ken, his accompanist, would arrive at his house at ten in the morning to go over songs and parodies he was planning to use. George kept his brain stimulated by going to Hillcrest Country Club in Los Angeles for lunch and sitting at what was called the comic's table—a place where old vaudevillians like Jack Benny, Groucho Marx, Henny Youngman, and others joined those they called the new boys: performers like Buddy Hackett, Don Rickles, and Bob Newhart. All of them would share jokes and amazing repartee, exercising their minds and testing new material.

Following a gin game, where he usually made money, Mr. Burns would go home for a nap and then, dressed to the nines for the evening and enjoying the company of women much younger, my friend could be found at dinner in one of Beverly Hills' swankiest restaurants, holding court.

This remarkable nonagenarian clearly understood the need to make challenge central to his life, even in his nineties. Sadly, George Burns did not quite make his hundredth birthday, but maybe there's a Caesar's Palace in heaven, where he's united with his wonderful wife, Gracie, and still working on material for the next act.

When writing this chapter, I sat for a long time pondering whether there was any challenge life could present that would not offer us the opportunity to overcome it and grow. Frankly, after careful consideration I cannot honestly find even a single one. I believe that life, through faith, offers eternal life after death,

> There is nothing in my time here on earth that cannot be managed into a positive.

and since that is central to my essence as a human being, there is nothing in my time here on earth that cannot be managed into a positive.

How often have you seen remarkable courage demonstrated during national disasters and heard people say that though they may have lost their homes, their property, and even loved ones, they treasure the goodness they have experienced through the help of others? That help serves as a reminder that love can overcome even the greatest tragedies.

I have had the distinct honor and pleasure of knowing thousands of people with disabilities, and so many of them have served as an inspiration to me in the way they have chosen to consistently affirm the idea that disability can be turned into ability. I've seen families split apart by divorce, where the parents actually become even more committed to their children and grow the relationships through the experience.

A few years ago I was fortunate to be a guest on *The Oprah Winfrey Show*. On that particular day I met a twelve-year-old boy, Mattie Stepanek, with muscular dystrophy. At twelve Mattie had already written two books of remarkable poetry and had a philosophy of life unlike anyone's I had ever known. He believed truly in the power of the mind and even more so in the power of prayer. He did not view his muscular dystrophy as a negative, but even at his young age he had already decided that it offered him the opportunity to be better than he might have been, had he been able to walk. Out of the limitations of his body had arisen the expansion of his mind and his capacity to communicate, both through his poetry and his dialogue with people much older than himself, reminding me of the young Jesus teaching the scribes and Pharisees in the temple.

Mattie's illness had certainly accelerated his acceptance of his challenge, and I suppose his race with time—a race he lost. If we acknowledge our finite existence on this blue ball spinning through space, should we not accept the idea that only through challenge do we grow and demonstrate the insight necessary for real happiness? Against the adversity of our challenges, we expand our mental, physical, and emotional horizons. Only against the crucible of challenge are we able to find out just how unique we are and how much we can accomplish by accepting the simple truth that challenge is the gateway to opportunity.

CHAPTER 17

The "It" Factor

I'LL BET THAT everyone reading this book has met a person or persons who has "it." But what is "it"? Like energy, it can't be created or destroyed. It's something that exists or doesn't in each person. We know that it's a force, a presence, a style, a something that certain people are gifted with and all of us instantly recognize.

It was 1957, and my father, who by the way had "it" in spades, took me out of school on the first Tuesday of April. And where do you think we went? Fenway Park to see the Red Sox begin their season against the dreaded Bronx Bombers, the New York Yankees—Mickey Mantle, Yogi Berra, and their great southpaw starting pitcher Whitey Ford.

Now, when you have the "it" factor working for you, you can be just about anything and get away with it. On this day my father bought tickets in Sun Bums Alley, the center field bleachers, that cost oh, something like a $1.25 apiece. But that's not where we went. I could hear that we got closer and closer to the field while batting practice was under way. And then I remember he opened a little door, and we stepped into a room with padded seats. It wasn't until the seventh inning, when a Boston cop told us we had to leave the owner's box, that I realized exactly where we were.

Yep. That's right. We were sitting in Tom Yawkey's box because my father knew from his Irish cronies that Yawkey never attended opening day but watched the game on television in the Statler Hotel. So, as far as my father, the larger-than-life Irishman with the "it" factor, was concerned, he and his little son could go sit anywhere they wanted, even the owner's box.

That wasn't all that happened on that most special day. I ate four hot dogs with everything on them, along with two bags of peanuts and three Cokes, and promptly got sick in the parking lot after the game. But during the experience it was all wonderful.

And the highlight for a father and a son occurred when the Splendid Splinter, Number 9, the greatest left-handed hitter in baseball history, John Wayne on spikes, who gave the best six years of his life in service to his country—Ted Williams— walked over to where we were sitting in the owner's box during batting practice to greet my father and his ecstatic little boy.

Now, my father may have had the "it" factor, but his star paled compared to the impression Ted Williams made on me. First, it was his voice. It boomed around the stadium.

"So, this is the lad," he said, dropping a huge arm around my shoulders. "This is the lad you've told me so much about, huh, Porky?"—my father's nickname. "Your dad tells me you love baseball, Tommy," he went on, "and that you know every batting average on the team. Is that right?"

You know what? Maybe I had a little of the "it" factor myself, because I went into a litany of everyone's lifetime batting average, including guys on the Red Sox who didn't even play very much.

Williams's laugh rang in the early spring air. "Well," he said, "maybe we could use a new manager around here. I don't think the one we've got knows as much about us as you do. What do you think, Porky? You think we can take Tommy out of school and give him a job?"

Now it was my father's turn to laugh.

Williams went on, "Well, maybe not a job, but I'll bet you'd like this, Tommy."

And there it was. Ted Williams took off his hat and placed that Red Sox hat on my head. It was pretty big and sort of drooped down over my whole face. But who cared? It was the great man's hat, and now I owned it. There was another hug, and Ted strolled back to take a few more warm-up swings, and I heard the crack as he hit three out over the Green Monster in left field.

What's important to note here is that it was not the stats that Ted Williams accumulated over twenty-one years in the majors that gave him the "it" factor. It was evident in the way he presented himself. Larger than life. Supremely confident. Certainly opinionated. Charismatic. Engaging. Dynamic. We can apply a lot of words that are part of the "it" factor, but essentially, in the case of the athlete, I think confidence is the most important aspect necessary in the way they apply themselves to their sport and to life.

Continuing in a sports motif, I have a terrific friend from down under in New Zealand named Rod Dixon. *Runner's World* has called him the greatest runner of the century, and for good reason. My friend Rod competed on five Olympic teams, and at different points in his running life he held world records in the fifteen hundred meters, three thousand meters, five thousand meters, ten thousand meters, and to put a topper on all of it, the New York Marathon. No other man in track history has come even close to his achievements.

But when we discuss the "it" factor that allowed him to do so much in a pair of Nikes, I want you to understand that what set him apart was the sheer joy he got out of running. His "it" factor, though supported by confidence, arose out of the absolute joy he took from the experience.

> His "it" factor arose out of absolute joy.

Rod grew up in Nelson, a small farming town on the South Island of New Zealand. He once told me that as a boy he would actually race across the fields chasing his shadow. Imagine that. Like a deer or an antelope or some other graceful animal, Rod chased his shadow, knowing he would never catch it, but engaged completely in the connection between mind and body as he raced the sun. Confidence and joy are two of the elements that frame the "it" factor.

And then there's communication: the ability to have an opinion and then make a point or argument that influences other people into either believing in your cause or, more importantly, believing in you.

No one has ever communicated more relevantly to so many at one time than the great communicator, President Ronald Reagan. I had the chance to meet our fortieth president on a number of occasions, and what struck me always was the warmth he exuded. In my case, though our meetings spanned a period of ten years, he never forgot my name, my wife's name, or anything we had spoken about in the past.

The second thing I was aware of was that even if our conversation was brief, the president talked only to me when we were having it. By that I mean to say his focus, which has often been questioned by the media, was never lacking. Certainly, I understand in his later years Alzheimer's robbed him of this very special gift, but in the multiple times I met him, his concentration on me and what we were sharing was absolute and very specific.

And when he gave a speech—wow. Just to be there, to experience a Reagan speech, was a remarkable event in my life that still has an impact on all of my beliefs today. I'm convinced that his gift of communication arose out of his commitment to the principles important to who he was.

President Reagan knew himself and understood the country in his own unique context. He completely believed in the American spirit and the limitless ability of Americans to overcome any national or international adversity. He was also a great storyteller, and the lilt of Irish humor was readily on his tongue.

If you're a great communicator and you support the gift with unwavering principles, you have "it."

If talent blends with a substantial work ethic, you also have "it," and no one that I've known exemplifies this idea better than the great Ella Fitzgerald.

> If talent blends with a substantial work ethic, you have "it."

I met Ella late in her life, when I was attending a party with Quincy Jones, the magnificent composer, arranger, conductor, and producer. Ella had heard me sing on *The Tonight Show* and surprised me by demanding to know why I wasn't singing more. I guess I stammered something about not having enough opportunity, but she wasn't buying it.

"Listen, Tom," she said, "you better be singing because you love it. Talent just isn't enough. It takes hard work and diligence. So, don't let me not hear that great voice of yours."

Beyond the compliment from Ella, I was touched by her intensity and learned later that this magnificent singer had begun her career as a dancer in Harlem and then moved to singing when she performed in an amateur show at the great Apollo Theater and won. Later on, when she was working with big bands like the Count Basie Orchestra, Ella actually went back to school and learned to read music. And not just read it. Musicians I've known told me over the years that Ella could read the fly specs on a page. By that I mean she could look at a score and follow all the instrument parts simultaneously in order to choose the riff that she was going to sing.

A consummate professional, Ella blended talent with a powerful work ethic, along with the confidence, joy, and communication skill to make her a great artist. If you do all that, it's easy for me to say you have the "it" factor.

My agent, Jan Miller, recently represented "Sully" Sullenberger, the pilot who landed an airplane on the Hudson River. We all remember the afternoon when it happened, and many of us were glued to our televisions as the amazing crew guided the crippled aircraft down onto the water.

Sullenberger told Jan that the descent and landing had to be extremely precise in order to place the airplane on the river tail first. "If it hit flat," he said, "she would have broken apart, so we really had to get the vectors just right."

Jan related that she asked Sullenberger about his emotions during the experience. He said it was only after the fact that he became frightened. "The tougher it got," he noted, "the more my training kicked in."

Certainly, there was no joy in this experience, except for the fact that everyone was rescued, but communication with others, along with the confidence to believe in his competence allowed him to land the plane safely, guaranteeing that all of the passengers would return to their families and loved ones. Boy, oh boy, that's competence—and that's a man with the "it" factor.

I don't know anyone as courageous as my friend Erik Weihenmayer, the blind man who climbed to the top of Mount Everest. Imagine that. Just try! A blind person conquering the highest mountain in the world.

He did it through hard work, climbing other mountains all over the world to prepare. In preparing well, he developed the confidence to believe that he could achieve this seemingly impossible feat. And in that satisfaction there truly was a level of joy. He had to communicate with the other climbers because clearly they don't know what it's like to be blind or what a blind person really needs. And they must believe in his competence, because he's not the only one on a belay line when they snake their way across an ice bridge and summit at better than twenty-three thousand feet.

My friend Erik is either the bravest person I've ever known or the craziest, but either way his courage is undaunted and unyielding. And he has a relentless "it" factor.

Okay, I could go on and on creating a litany of parts that make up the elements found in the "it" factor, but I think you get the point. Depending on the individual, the "it" factor can arise from many different fountains of human capacity. Its essence can come from a person's courage or the joy they get from doing the thing they love.

Competence can engender the "it" factor because we see it in others and feel safe, and to be able to communicate effectively creates the potential for leadership. Without exception, all leaders possess the "it" factor, but it doesn't necessarily mean they're demonstrative or even socially comfortable.

Think about the technology revolution and how we generally apply the term *geek* to those people who have created it. In their way, they have to be able to inspire, drawing others into their vision and creating companies that have changed the landscape of global business.

The "it" factor can be found in all sizes, shapes, and types of human beings. They can be shy or dominant. They can motivate others or just be aggressive self-starters who work alone and inspire by example. But there is one central theme that permeates all of the people who possess the "it" factor: every one of them, without any exception, is a visionary.

Now, I do need to qualify this idea by saying that sometimes the vision is limited to only the person's own specific desires. In the case of many of my friends who are actors, I have found them to be people who are completely self-absorbed and single-focused. To be fair, I'm not sure they have much choice. A career in show business is dog-eat-dog, and it's extremely tough to think outside of your own sphere when you're chasing such an elusive dream. But single-focused visionaries really get it done.

Early in my career I met the great Orson Welles and was amazed at his sense that he was simply the greatest actor in the history of the American stage. Many biographers have recorded how difficult he could be to work with, but no one can deny the significance of many of his films and radio broadcasts.

The movie *Citizen Kane* will stand forever as a piece of springing vision, and its undeniable star, Orson Welles, clearly used the power of the "it" factor to give us one of the great movie treasures of our time.

Even when the vision is limited by self-absorption or is as broad as those people who believe they can change the world, the "it" factor can only be maintained and expanded if the people who have it are real visionaries.

So, we come to the question of whether the "it" factor can be developed. I think the jury's out on that. I've seen many people gain a competence that translates to confidence, provides joy, and really does engage others in a way that seems incongruous when considering the person who's moving the needle.

A number of my friends tell me, as an example, that Warren Buffett is one of the most low-key, humble human beings they've ever been around, and yet no one in the history of global finance has had more impact on economic growth, vision, or corporate stability than this great financier.

So, I guess we come back to exactly where we were at the beginning of this chapter. The "it" factor is a force drifting in space just waiting to attach itself to the hopes, dreams, and passions of particular human beings. While I'm not sure whether it can be developed, I'm sure it can become part of people whose emotional perspective ranges all over the human spectrum.

The "it" factor is a force just waiting
to attach itself to the dreams
of particular human beings.

If you're a person possessing the "it" factor, be grateful for it. And if you're someone who believes that it's not part of your personality, go out and attach yourself, your dreams, your desires, your passions to a person who has this most remarkable gift. These are the leaders, the people who stand out from the crowd, the humans who make the biggest difference. But remember, even though they may be the brightest star in the night sky, they need interdependent team members to make the greatest impact.

The world needs more people with the "it" factor, but we also need others who support it and help it grow.

CHAPTER 18

Vision Statement

I LIKE THE WAY I see the world. No, that's not really quite the truth. I love the way I see the world, and I'm finally at a place in my life where I no longer envy those of you with traditional external vision. Again, let me reiterate that I would love to see my wife's face, see my children's smiles, or stand on top of the cliff near my Palos Verdes home in California looking out at the surf at the end of a day and maybe watching one of our incredible sunsets. But I'm at peace about the fact that I can't see those things.

> I no longer envy those of you with traditional external vision.

My friend Derek Gill, the man I wrote my first book with, *If You Could See What I Hear*, once described a sunset for me as listening to panes of glass shatter. He said that if you took the glass and broke it, letting it fall from a great height, the sound would be like the myriad of colors in the spectrum of light at the end of a perfect day. I don't get it. My friend was amazingly articulate, and yet this image just doesn't connect for me. Neither does the concept of color.

Often people have tried to compare sound to color, in hopes that I might understand, and as I said in an earlier chapter I have no picture of dimension other than being able to touch an object with my hands or walk around a large space.

I'm noting all of these things in retrospect because my awareness will never change, and that sunset, that rainbow, those colors, that special face are things I'll never see, but if this book has had any purpose contained in its pages, it's in my hope that you can grow and expand your knowledge of the world by expanding your vision to be inside out.

I did not write this book as a how-to but more as a work of observation. However, as we frame this last chapter, let me take a little time to make positive suggestions as to the *how* of inner vision. There is an amazing potential for expanding our sensory awareness. This is one area where just by simply deciding you can expand your sensory skill by quantum leaps.

Why not practice closing your eyes and sitting outside on a summer morning, determining how many sounds you can hear just by choosing to pay attention? In my own environment I often have counted how many different birdsongs touch my heart and lift my spirit. Most particularly, I love robins. I don't know if it's a throwback to the way I grew up in New England when that first spring robin meant that the seasons were about to change, or whether it's because I love the warble of their tune, but I know for sure that listening to morning birds has always been spiritually uplifting and a terrific way to begin a positive day.

That's the point of our senses in general. They are tools that provide us with the good things of life, and all of them can be sharpened. Remember that I spoke about the game my children and I used to play called "What's Mommy Doing?" When Patty would be in the kitchen and Blythe and Tom would use their olfactory talents to determine what was going on out there? Touch and taste can generate so much information that you overlook with your eyes, and I believe you will be amazed at the increased capacity for sensory awareness that can be gained just by saying "I'll try it, I'll practice." Just by saying yes.

> Senses are tools that provide us with the good things of life.

It's just as easy and just as exciting to explore the question of true beauty. For thousands of years men and women have created archetypes, artistic images for physical beauty, but very little time has been invested on a true evaluation of the far more important context of internal beauty that shines out as vivid as an Arizona sunrise. Why Arizona? Because that's where Patty is from, and like the early morning light there is not a day when I don't feel the embrace of her internal beauty. Because of who she is I'm becoming my best self. Beauty, you see, can be reflected like an internal mirror from one human being to another, and I have been made a better person because of who she is and will always be in my life.

The acceptance of beauty discovered from inside out also allows us to eliminate the scourge of labels. It's profoundly lazy when we categorize our fellow man according to labels. It means we are not looking deep enough, not caring enough to find out more about the people we come in contact with. Sadly, we have fought wars over labels. Often they are concepts that were determined thousands of years before. Wars over religion or race are certainly the worst aspect of how we label each other, and frankly I don't see it changing in the future.

The most insidious application of labels arises out of the worst of who we are as a species. We want to brand. We seem to have a tragic need to indicate our own superiority by labeling the other. And I pray that my insight in this book on the adoption of labels will, in a small way, cause you to reconsider every encounter and every relationship.

This is a good time for me to tell you that I believe people are wonderful, and when I wrote about the people who have changed my life I was only giving you a representative sample because, simply put, I love human beings. We are the most interesting and complex of God's creations, and it is so much fun to get to know as many as possible.

As I'm writing, I'm realizing that every once in a while I need to go back and make a connection. We learn about beauty and the world around us through our senses, and the habit of being open to the possibilities externally allows us to internalize the elimination of labels and the joy we experience getting to know the people we contact on our life's journey. It's all part of the mosaic of twenty-twenty inside-out vision.

When these pieces are in place operationally, it's not a hard leap to begin to believe that all disadvantages can be turned into advantages, and an open heart and nature can turn any relationship into a useful positive.

A glass-half-full philosophy, rather than glass-half-empty, comes about when we assume that every life experience can be expanded into positive advantages. I don't care if people believe this sounds Pollyannaish. I don't mind because I'm loving the whole process of being alive.

> I'm loving the whole
> process of being alive.

Now, there are moments that test my beliefs. I call them turning points, and they define our characters, but again the linkage is clear. If we are convinced that disadvantage can be turned into advantage, then turning points serve as the crucibles that allow us to become better people.

Here's another connection. If character is tested at turning-point moments, how is it evaluated? Bingo! By the man in the mirror. When we demonstrate the willingness to take a good look at ourselves, at who we really are and how we treat others, we are able to define our character, and it's at this juncture of awareness that we examine our purpose for being.

Are we purposeful? That was a question I raised, but we define that most important idea when we examine the man in the mirror. To be a purposeful human being, to be of good purpose—that is essential, and it's a question I ask myself repeatedly. The answer is founded in the premise that as long as I'm sure that I am relating to you selflessly, rather than out of my own selfish desires, I'm living as a person of good purpose.

And what is the instrument that drives this equation? It is our passion, our willingness to apply that passion on behalf of the people we encounter and the purpose we have designed. Passion implies risk because to announce where you are coming from to the other suggests that they're willing to accept your idea, or at least tolerate it.

I have often been accused of being too

> As long as I am relating to
> you selflessly, I'm living as
> a person of good purpose.

passionate, and I suppose some of my critics have a good point. I'm over the top when it comes to passion. I admit it. But for the most part it is geared toward expanding the common good, that is, what I believe is good for me and good for you.

With the application of purposeful passion, an important insight to be aware of is how much satisfaction—no, that is not a big enough word—how much fantastic joy life offers. It's not unreasonable to say that each of us should have the right to feel proud of our involvement with others. By that I mean not simply proud of our accomplishments but proud of the responsibility entailed by being willing to become a leader. If you choose to lead others, you must accept the responsibility for your actions.

That's why I define *pride* as Personal Responsibility for Individual Daily Effort. Call it our conscience, the consciousness necessary to step out there and support our inside-out beliefs. The application of our character to every situation that touches our lives needs to operate from personal responsibility for any individual daily effort, or

> I'm convinced that every person, within their own life context, can be a winner.

pride. Though it sometimes can resonate as false or ego-driven, when applied in this way, pride is a testimony to all winners, and at my core I'm convinced that every person, within their own life context, can be a winner. There are choices to be made, but those choices are not abstract. They're concepts available to all of us.

A clear example is the discussion earlier in this book on being handi-capable rather than handicapped or abled versus disabled.

Your physical circumstance is not the determining factor in whether you view yourself as abled or disabled, and there is clearly a major decision to be made. I'm not suggesting that 54 million Americans with significant disabilities can change their futures in a day or just because they decide to improve their circumstance. It takes hard work and the cooperation of every person and community, but I am sure that we all have the capacity to be part of the solution.

When I wrote the chapter on reality, I laid out a strong case for change, and I believe change is necessary, but at the core of my being, and as an absolute commitment in the way I choose to use my inner vision, I live every day with the idea that change is possible. More than possible, it is probable. And I believe it because of another concept

> We will not succeed as a global community unless we are willing to accept the concept of interdependence.

central to life as I see it. It is in the premise I suggested of independence, dependence, and interdependence. We will not succeed as a society, or certainly, now more than ever, as a global community, unless we are willing to accept the concept of interdependence.

The microcosm in my life from which this theory developed is accurate in every human relationship, from the most personal in our family units to the largest international stage of nation-to-nation building. Individuals, families, tribes, societies, nations, and the world have proved it over and over and over again in the pantheon of history: societies that lack interdependence inevitably fail. It is only when the theory of interdependence becomes the foundation of enlightenment that hope for a bright future can take root, flourish, and grow.

Let me say that I'm not blind to these ideas. My mind's eye is wide open, and my vision is twenty-twenty, and there is nothing written in any of these pages that I don't believe. Why? Because of my faith in Him. A higher power, God the Father, who in His love is providing all of us with the grace to become one with Him forever and ever, amen.

I hope as you read this work you're saying quietly to yourself, *Wow, I'm not even using half of my potential. There's so much more available for me to try, to experience, to appreciate, to see.*

If you're saying these things, then this book is a success. Remember, you have the unlimited capacity to utilize all of your inner-vision skills and experience all of life. And isn't that wonderful?

The old hymn is applicable for me in every way as the epigraph for this work: "I once was lost but now am found, was blind, but now I see."

Epilogue

I WAS EXCITED, really excited, because I had been invited back to Perkins School for the Blind in Watertown, Massachusetts, the place that I had certainly not embraced as a child but had come to believe was a magnificent institution of love and education for blind children from around the world. In fact, over the years, Perkins had expanded its reach to over sixty countries with important satellite programs for blind children on all parts of the globe.

I was going to give a concert for the board of directors and their families, teachers, staff, and most importantly, the students; and Perkins had a big surprise for me. They invited all of the people that had graduated in my class in 1965, friends I hadn't seen for over forty-seven years. The school arranged for all of us to share a cocktail party before my performance—just us, forty or so blind people who had experienced almost no contact during all those years.

I wondered before the gathering what it would be like. Would we all seem old? Would we have aged in ways that made recognizing each other impossible? Had we grown in so many different directions that we would have nothing in common?

My concerns certainly weren't validated. From the second we entered the room and began the process of handshakes and hugs, time was no longer a factor, age was not a factor, life circumstances were no factor. We were ageless, timeless. We were the same people who had loved and shared, been educated and grown. Most significantly to us we looked exactly the same, though to the observer our external appearances had completely changed. Our inside-out vision of each other was forever the same.

So, as I see it, my friend Phyllis Mitchell is still beautiful. Her hair isn't gray because her personality shines through. As I see it, my friend Bobby is just as enthused as he always was. Charlie is just as funny, and Paul is still smarter than the rest of us.

As I see it, we are the same, and though I acknowledge that's only my impression, the idea that I can hold friendship in a time capsule, that people could stay the way they always had been, is the greatest gift of inside-out vision. As I see it, my friends are still God's beautiful creations—enthusiastic, passionate, energized, joyous, loving, special, and oh, by the way, blind. The same twenty-twenty vision that has made my life spectacular can enrich all of you with a new way of seeing. So, open your mind's eye and see where it leads.

Afterword

WHAT'S THAT OLD PHRASE? *I'm looking at the world through rose-colored glasses.* I guess that means seeing the world only the way you want to see it. And certainly, in these pages I'm suggesting an approach to inside-out vision that has been built around both the way I see life and the way I guess I want it to be.

Whenever you're writing a book, before you send it to your editor, some authors want to build up their confidence by asking some people they respect to read an early draft. In this case, I had given the manuscript to some selected friends with disabilities because I was curious to find out how they felt about my approach to vision.

Now, I also gave it to some people who were not directly disabled, and their feelings came back exactly the way I expected. They were surprised and, thankfully, excited about the possibilities of expanding their own sense of sight. But from my disabled friends I got some very interesting commentary. One note particularly from a young guy who is multidisabled really stopped me in my tracks.

"Dude," he said.

I always like it when young people call me *dude*.

"Dude, you're looking at all of this through rose-colored glasses, and I think you'd better get a handle on the reality of the role our disabilities play out there in the world. I mean, I suppose it's great for you to think the way you do, but I think you ought to take some time and reflect on the fact that society isn't as open to your kind of vision as you seem to think."

As I considered what he said, I could certainly understand where he was coming from. There are 54 million disabled people in America, and though great progress has been made over the last twenty years in terms of creating an equal playing field, my friend's reality check is important for me to both acknowledge and talk about. Though every idea I've represented in these pages is absolutely a concept I truly believe in, certainly the way disabled people are treated by the public at large does both cloud and, yes, confuse the potential of having inside-out vision.

In recent decades, two important pieces of legislation were created to change the lives of disabled people. The Americans with Disabilities Act and the Equal Educational Opportunities Act became law. In principle these guaranteed virtually complete access to all rights necessary for the disabled to create the freedom they deserve, and former senator Robert Dole, a disabled veteran himself, and others who pioneered this important legislation deserve great credit.

But laws don't necessarily present opportunity for systems if small minds are closed to the possibilities. Though equal education of all Americans is now mandated, the success of individual programs has been profoundly disappointing. Concepts like mainstreaming and inclusion are great, but intent has little to do with effective execution.

After years of observing special education classes in public schools, I'd like to describe what I usually found on American school campuses. In theory, we're supposed to see children with all levels of disability participating in as many standard class programs as possible. The reality is that in most cases a special education teacher operates his or her classroom with a mixed bag of disabilities all brought together and isolated with a number of well-meaning aides trying to support this overworked specialist to provide individual programs for every special-needs child. The composition of her classroom may have two Down syndrome kids, two or three blind kids, a couple of deaf kids, some wheelchair-bound children—oh, and let's just throw in some autism to make it even more complex—along with a coterie of other disabilities I'm not even naming. This special education teacher is simply overwhelmed, and because of the separation of her classroom from the student population, disabled children are rarely able to bridge the social gaps necessary to take their rightful place as participating members of this school community.

Obviously, I know a lot more about the state of blindness in education than any other disability, so let me talk to you about an area in which I really am an expert. In the eighties there was a great move to place as many blind children as possible in public schools. I was all for it. I even campaigned through commercials and television appearances all over the country to make it happen. Unfortunately, the experiment has been a total bust, and now many of the bright young blind people with limitless potential I hoped would find their place with their sighted peers have returned to state schools for the blind, believing that the education opportunities in these institutions are far greater than the isolation created by mainstream student programs.

Certainly, a lot of this arises out of real budget limitations, so finding enough special education teachers who can move from school to school and engage the blind student population throughout a school district is a real concern. The future of all blind children is going to be largely based on the willingness of the parents to keep pushing the system so that it provides the children they love with every option available.

Under the Education Act, every student with a disability is to be guaranteed an IEP (Individual Education Plan) to move them forward on an appropriate academic track. Again, the intention is laudable, but with so many children involved, these meetings often are much too short, and the follow-up just doesn't occur.

In a typical IEP session the principal, teacher, parents, counselors, and any additional therapists, both emotional and physical, who are involved in the child's life come together and try to hash out the good, bad, and ugly of what's happening to Johnny. Again, terrific conceptually, but when Johnny returns to the special education classroom, all the pieces simply don't fall into place, and much of what Johnny needs gets lost. We see a classroom setting where aides the school provided for Johnny only visit him once a week because of the extraordinary demands placed on limited resources. Also, Johnny is faced with the hubbub of a special education classroom where all the children with various disabilities struggle to gain the attention they need. Consequently, Johnny's ability to concentrate, to focus, to grow, and to thrive is extraordinarily limited.

Now I have many, many heroes involved in special education. From principals to teachers, social workers to superintendents of schools, I know great human beings working to make a difference on behalf of disabled children and their families; but the system is breaking down and, frankly, getting much worse. In the world of blindness, for example, according to a study done by the American Foundation for the Blind, over 30 percent of the children who are attending public school programs have returned to state schools for the blind in order to gain the support they need.

And what about our adult population? Where are they in the second decade of the twenty-first century? Here's the alarming statistic. According to the National Council on Disability, of the 30 million disabled people with the capacity to hold meaningful employment, only 12 percent have jobs. Everyone else is either dependent on their families or receiving SSI support from the government. Of all the elements that blur my vision and fill my eyes with tears, this statistic is the most upsetting.

Looking at the system collectively, it seems that those people with exceptional talent can rise above adversity, and I must also say that for those special-needs folks whose disability is profound, the system in general does a pretty good job. The breakdown largely affects those who fall somewhere in the middle—people with major disability but average ability. Training programs and individual support just do not exist with a presence that can change the status quo.

Systems can only do so much. If my vision for the future of disabled Americans is going to become clear, if the haze is going to be lifted and a rainbow of promise shines through, individuals—you and me and every other American citizen—will need to be willing to step up and make a difference. And it doesn't take much if each of us just does a little.

Why not expose your children to a disabled child? Create a social interaction. I think you'll find that your little person will be much better off because of the experience. If you're involved in community programs with your own kids, make sure you find a way to integrate the organization with programs for the disabled. Even though the law requires access, it takes a parent willing to get involved to make the critical difference in their child's participation.

In the workplace, why not ask your corporation what kind of training they offer for people with special needs? And if there isn't any, hey, make a little noise and create one.

Here's the big payoff. The truth is a handout can be a hand up. In this population of 54 million disabled people, there are so many human beings with remarkable gifts to offer you if they can just gain the exposure, the access to celebrate their own specialness and allow us to benefit from the qualities that make them wonderful.

So, to my disabled friends who rightfully critiqued my pages, thank you. I'm taking off my rose-colored glasses and opening my eyes wide to the reality of disability in America. At the same time, my inside-out vision has made me—and I'm not embarrassed to say this—an ultimate optimist. I believe in the capacity of human beings to do almost anything if they choose to, and I believe in the unlimited passion of the human spirit to never view anything as impossible. I also am very sure that the courage and strength I've found in so many of my friends with disability will find its place if they're only given a fair chance.

Remember that earlier in this work I expressed my opinion that everyone in the world has a disability and that the key to being a successful human being is to turn your disability into ability. I have lived my entire adult life believing in this formula, and I'm much too old to give up the idea now. And so, my vision is very clear when I look at the future for me and the millions of other disabled people.

The legal system has provided us with the rights under the law we need to find our footing in the world. Now it's up to your goodwill and our hard work. Let's reach out and do it together.

About the Author

Tom Sullivan is an actor, singer, entertainer, author, and producer. When he was born prematurely in 1947, he was given too much oxygen while in an incubator. Though it saved his life, it cost him his eyesight. The "inconvenience" of being blind has never kept Tom from competing in a world where he realized that to be equal, for him, meant that he must be better. Tom's guest stints on television led to two Emmy nominations. As a special correspondent for ABC's *Good Morning America*, Tom was a regular morning fixture in millions of American homes. A major motion picture was made of his life based on his autobiography, *If You Could See What I Hear,* starring Marc Singer. Tom is now writing and producing for television and film. He is the author of fiction, nonfiction, and children's books.